# *Winning the war with bipolar*

Samuel J. Swidzinski

Copyright © 2020 by Samuel J. Swidzinski

All rights reserved. No part of this book may be reproduced or used in any manner without written permission of the copyright owner except for the use of quotations in a book review. Please email samuel.swidzinski@kcl.ac.uk for any questions.

FIRST EDITION

# DISCLAIMER

Hi, I'm Sam, and I'm diagnosed with bipolar 1 disorder. This book discusses my personal experience and personal opinions about bipolar. I'm not a clinical psychologist or psychiatrist.

This book isn't intended as a substitute for medical care. Before changing your lifestyle in any way, you should consult a physician or other licenced healthcare professional.

This book provides information on my own experience of mental health issues. Use of this book implies your acceptance of this disclaimer.

# ACKNOWLEDGMENTS

I want to express gratitude to the friends and family that have helped me in both my recovery and the process of writing this book.

Primarily, I would like to acknowledge with gratitude the support and love of my parents, Anna and Richard; my sisters, Zosia, Laura and Linka; my nephews, Max, Seb and Jacob; my girlfriend, Pricilla Lam; and my friends, Daniel Paget, Kalena Lilla and Zak Zourdani. Without the support of my family and friends, I doubt I would be alive today. Their support is so much appreciated.

Many thanks to Dr Sameer Jauhar, Hayley Montgomery, Dr Frances Meeten, Dr Jennifer Rusted, Natalia Griffiths and Chinezuizo Maduakor for their support. There are many other people who deserve my thanks; however, the list would soon become too long and tiresome to read.

## SPECIAL MENTION

A dear friend of mine, George Dee, deserves a special mention for helping me in the process of editing and producing this book. Without his support, this book wouldn't have been nearly as fun to write, the journey would have been far more difficult, and my motivation would have been considerably lowered.

# Table of Contents

**PREFACE**
My Graduation.................................................................1

**CHAPTER I**
A war within the mind....................................................5

**CHAPTER II**
You deserve to have someone tell you: "You are worthy and you are awesome."...................................9

## Section 1:
What is bipolar disorder?..............................................13

**CHAPTER III**
The misconceptions surrounding bipolar… are bipolar............................................................................15

**CHAPTER IV**
Mania and Hypomania: Part 1: People pay a lot of money to feel the way I do. But should they?............28

**CHAPTER V**
The Symptoms of Depression: My own experience.....53

**CHAPTER VI**
Mixed episodes and rapid cycling – How am I going to survive this one?.......................................................63

**CHAPTER VII**
What have we learnt here?...........................................67

## Section 2:
*How to make the best of therapy*..................69

**CHAPTER VIII**
Why doesn't therapy work for me?...............71

**CHAPTER IX**
Go for the right reasons..................................73

**CHAPTER X**
Rapport: It's not just about 'getting on' with your therapist..........................................................76

**CHAPTER XI**
Don't go when in the midst of an episode: Especially not a manic one!..............................82

**CHAPTER XII**
What is the therapy about?............................87

**CHAPTER XIII**
Do the homework...........................................91

**CHAPTER XIV**
Your therapy blueprint is your best friend...97

**CHAPTER XV**
Why did some of my psychiatrists benefit me and others not?...................................................102

## Section 3:
*How to become your own psychologist*...........107

**CHAPTER XVI**
Know your illness, know yourself and know the difference between the two...........109

**CHAPTER XVII**
Journaling...........117

**CHAPTER XVIII**
Know your triggers...........123

**CHAPTER XIX**
Action plans: Know how to respond...........127

**CHAPTER XX**
Manage Stress...........132

**CHAPTER XXI**
Manage Anger...........138

**CHAPTER XXII**
Embrace Vulnerability...........143

**CHAPTER XXIII**
Replace Shame with Empathy...........146

**CHAPTER XXIV**
Manage healthy attachments...........149

**CHAPTER XXV**
Manage social circle...........153

**CHAPTER XXVI**
Building our metacognitive abilities...........156

**CHAPTER XXVII**
Getting Structure Back in My Life ................................ 163

**CHAPTER XXVIII**
Working on my life goals ............................................. 168

**CHAPTER XXIX**
Slow and steady wins the race ..................................... 171

## *Section 4:*
*Consistency, Consistency and more Consistency* ...... 175

**CHAPTER XXX**
Why is consistency so important? ............................... 177

**CHAPTER XXXI**
Consistency in medication .......................................... 179

**CHAPTER XXXII**
Consistency in relapse prevention .............................. 185

**CHAPTER XXXIII**
Consistency in our relationships ................................. 190

**CHAPTER XXXIV**
Consistency despite hardships .................................... 197

**CHAPTER XXXV**
Consistency in my life goals ....................................... 203

**CHAPTER XXXVI**
A Note to those with bipolar disorder: Please remember that you are worthy and that you are awesome ..................................................................... 211

**CHAPTER XXXVII**
My Dad's Speech: To all the loved ones and mental health professionals out there ................................... 213

References ..................................................................... 216
AUTHOR BIO ................................................................ 222

# PREFACE
## *My Graduation*

Five years ago, I couldn't read a single page of a book. My bipolar disorder had stolen my ability to concentrate, remember what I had just read, or feel any motivation. Now, I'm able to write a book and pursue a PhD. I can't believe the transformation. If I could have seen a snapshot of myself as I'm now back then, I would say it's impossible, and this can't possibly be my future. For the majority of my teens and early twenties, my mood ranged from extreme highs to extreme lows with very few periods of stability. I didn't find the right treatment for a long time, and I saw no way of escaping this beast called bipolar.

My family held a party for me after graduating from University as they were so happy that I was finally able to function and excel. There were some tears and many smiles as we all thought of where I had been and where I was now. I wasn't alone in believing that this transformation was impossible. My family couldn't believe it either. I had gone from not being able to read a book to writing one. I had gone from having no hope, to helping others see hope within their futures. I had gone from the person who caused a lot of pain and stress in the lives of those I love, to trying to help the ones I love on their stressful journeys.

My Dad made a fantastic speech. He was a bit tipsy, and it was embarrassing at the time but heartfelt. He began by mentioning two individuals to whom I should be eternally grateful for my recovery. I agree entirely that, without these two people in my life, I wouldn't be where I am now. First, he thanked a research psychiatrist, Sameer, who helped me see the right professionals, get on the right medication and, most importantly, accept myself for who I am. He then mentioned my Mum, who has always been there for me, helping me to manage my medication and supporting me in times of need. The network I had around me was the foundation that allowed me to develop into the person I am today. I realise that many aren't as fortunate as I am to have had a support network to fall back on during their battle with bipolar.

Following this, my father said, 'But it was you that did the work'. He told me how proud he is of all the effort I've made to get to where I am today. I feel both proud and grateful for the life I have now. I feel comfortable with myself and in my social circle. I believe once we overcome a challenge as difficult as bipolar disorder, life looks much more colourful. It's as if my illness made me colour-blind, and now I am finally able to appreciate all the colours in my life.

Due to the knowledge passed down to me from far wiser people and through the many mistakes I've made on my journey, I have developed a pretty solid understanding of myself, my illness and the techniques that I needed to use to manage it. This book isn't the story of my life with bipolar disorder. It is a structured book, outlining the techniques that I've used to win my war against bipolar. I give the example of my own experience in my explanation of how these methods helped me. I also describe what bipolar disorder is, exposing some myths and showing how the symptoms often manifest in reality.

Perhaps you are reading this book because you, or someone you love, suffers from bipolar disorder. Maybe a diagnosis has already been made, or perhaps you have a nagging feeling that this disorder is the root cause of the psychological troubles afflicting you. Perhaps you are a psychologist or psychiatrist, wanting to see a patient's perspective on this complex and often misunderstood disorder. Or maybe you're simply interested in the topic of bipolar.

I am writing this book from the perspective of 'we' as I am part of the group who are diagnosed with this disorder. I write in this style to reassure all those who have this illness that they are not alone in this journey. However, regardless of your reasons for choosing this book, I welcome you and I hope that you can learn from my personal journey and that it can inspire you in some way.

# CHAPTER I
## *A war within the mind*

When at war, we are forced into many battles. Each one leaves us with scars, some of which we must carry with us forever. Sadly, some battle wounds cut so deep that we lose our lives. Each battle is unique. Some are more difficult than others. We have to adapt our strategies and approaches to the different battles that we are forced into. We fight to survive. We change.

Over time, war becomes the new norm. We even forget what life was like prior to the war and can't imagine living without it. Yet one day, the war does end. We take a while to readjust to ordinary life but once we do, we can cherish life all the more. A deep tranquillity resides within us because we know how much better life is now than it was before. We see the beauty in the little things that others don't because we know what life is like without them.

I've heard mental illness be likened to a war within the mind. I can deeply relate to this comparison. Many battles, otherwise known as episodes, that I have fought against bipolar disorder have left me with scars that I can still feel today. In some episodes, I almost lost my life to suicide. Battling took all of my time and energy, leaving no room to develop myself, work, build healthy relationships or study. I thought I would always be a slave to this disorder, forever in the clutches of an episode, without achieving any level of success in my life. Thankfully, with a great support team around me and vital intel gathered from far wiser people than myself, I have managed to beat bipolar disorder and win the war.

When I say that I've 'won the war' against bipolar, I don't mean that I've been cured or have found the cure. I've learnt how to manage this disorder well enough that I'm not only able to function well in life, but am, more importantly, able to say that I enjoy being alive. For the first time in forever, I love myself. I feel comfortable in who I am and am happy about the journey I am going on. I finally see all the colours that the world has to offer.

Today, I'm proud to be a mental health advocate and am grateful for the opportunity to research the effect of cognitive remediation therapy (CRT) on bipolar disorder. I'm thankful to a research psychiatrist, Sameer, who took me under his wing and helped me access the right support. He has inspired me to pursue a career in research. I wanted to empower people like he empowered me and to help them enjoy a meaningful life.

In my pursuit of gaining knowledge about bipolar disorder, I have engaged in many awesome conversations with psychiatric and psychological researchers. They have been very kind to me, and listening to their wisdom has helped me profoundly in my life. One piece of wisdom that has been particularly beneficial to my understanding of how to recover is regarding how to make therapy work. Here are the wise words that were passed on to me:

The relationship between a therapist and a client is like that of a teacher and a pupil. A teacher can't take exams for a student. The teacher's role is to help their students to (1) understand the subject matter (2) teach the techniques needed to pass the exam and (3) explain how and why those techniques work. If the student is able to understand these three steps, then they would be able to ace the exam themselves. Sometimes they may encounter new problems and may need help again to understand new concepts. However, if they understand the subject matter in-depth through their own persistent effort and through the help of their teacher, they can, one day, get to a point where they are able to overcome new problems without further assistance.

The therapy room isn't a place where we pass our exams. We won't finish therapy and have our problems disappear. But, if we understand our mental health disorder and how it works, know the techniques needed to manage symptoms and prevent relapse and understand how and why these techniques work, we can get to a point where we live a life without being burdened by our mental state. This is the stage that we should all aim to get to regarding our own psychology. This book shows the techniques that I've personally used on my road to recovery. We will be going through, in-depth, the four steps that I've used to get to this place of stability:

1. I now understand what bipolar is, how it works and what the medications do.
2. I know how to find the right therapist or psychiatrist for me and how to make the best of those relationships.
3. I have become my own psychologist.
4. I am consistent in my recovery journey and life goals.

Important to the journey is learning our worth. Prolonged and untreated bipolar disorder can eat away at our self-esteem. We will begin by explaining that all those with bipolar are capable, worthy, and deserve to live a good life.

# CHAPTER II
## *You deserve to have someone tell you: "You are worthy and you are awesome."*

When I was 18 years old, in my final year of school, I wanted some money. In the first mental health service that I went to, I came across some advertisements requesting volunteers to take part in research trials at Kings College London. The money they were offering participants wasn't huge, but I thought it would be an easy way to get some cash and also give me the opportunity to discuss mental health topics with some knowledgeable clinicians.

I took part in several trials in the coming months and greatly enjoyed meeting numerous researchers at Kings College. They had that look in their eyes where you could tell they really cared about what they were doing and, for the first time in my life, I felt heard by mental health professionals. They may not have been my assigned psychiatrists or psychologists, but their words of wisdom helped me a lot more than the mental health teams assigned to my care. This is because I felt that they truly cared about me, while also showing me a tremendous amount of respect.

I met Sameer, a specialist in bipolar disorder, in April of 2014. One day, we were sitting in a taxi as I was being transported to St Thomas' hospital to undergo an MRI scan. I asked him whether it would be possible for me to live a happy and productive life. In response, he smiled. He told me that he saw a lot of potential in me personally and mentioned that he believed people with bipolar disorder possess a vast amount of talent. He said that if we learn to manage our illness, we could become truly influential people and live a happy and full life.

He mentioned Dr Kay Jamison as an example of someone that suffered from a deep and painful bipolar disorder. She overcame it, becoming a prominent mental health advocate and psychologist who is respected worldwide. He said that he saw the potential in me to become like her one day and that he sees a great number of prospects and capabilities in all of us with bipolar.

Many of us only believe that we are capable and worthy when we are in a manic or hypomanic episode; when we feel high on life and full of energy. For this reason, a lot of us long for and search for these highs, even though they are painful and harmful in some ways. I've definitely done this in the past. In periods of depression and even in periods of stability, I would hope for a manic episode to come. When I could feel the onset of a manic episode, I would do nothing to prevent it. What I learned from Sameer, and through my own recovery experience, was that it isn't hypomania or mania that makes me capable. I can, and anyone with bipolar can achieve great things by having the determination to win this war, to fail at times but persist and come out of it a strong and wise individual.

Individuals with severe mental disorders such as bipolar or autism are often portrayed in the media as geniuses. Numerous studies have provided some validation to this claim, (Hankir, 2011); (Greenwood, 2016). In my opinion, this conception isn't due to the disorders, it is rather in spite of them. The ability to succeed greatly in life, for the most part, comes from work ethic. No matter how talented anyone is, without effort, we can't expect to achieve anything. One thing that unites us with those with autism is an obsessional nature. We exude a passion which can be applied to any goal or vision that we want to strive for. Once we manage our illness, we are able to strive towards our goals without interruption and achieve great things.

Also, the more anyone suffers in life, the more they are able to experience empathy. The skill of understanding the feelings of others is enhanced by our own experiences, (Lim & DeSteno, 2016). The more of a range of experiences we have, both internally and externally, the more we're able to relate to those around us. After overcoming bipolar, we can develop deep empathy for others. I know that, over the years, I haven't always been as kind to people as I wish I had been. I've made many mistakes and have sadly hurt a lot of people. But through those mistakes and through my own pain, I'm now able to fully love and show love to those around me.

I want to say to all of you with bipolar disorder, I believe in you. I believe in you to overcome this war within you and achieve great things. I believe in you to succeed in your goals and to develop deep, meaningful relationships. You are worthy. You have been dealt a difficult hand, but that doesn't take away from your worth and beauty.

In summary, the best philosophy that Sameer taught me was that, when I am able to overcome this massive hurdle, I will be able to accomplish anything in my life. I hope that the words in this book can inspire at least one person to take the next steps to attain the life they deserve; a life of joy, autonomy and success.

# Section 1:
# What is bipolar disorder?

# CHAPTER III
## *The misconceptions surrounding bipolar... are bipolar.*

I am very happy that there has been a marked improvement recently in mental health awareness globally. Stigma is decreasing, and many people who used to feel ashamed of their mental health are now advocates, proud of the battles that they have been fighting. Many of these mental health advocates dedicate their lives to helping others feel proud of themselves too. Is there still a lot of work to do in this area? Of course. Negative views on mental health are still rampant. A lot of people still feel ashamed for experiencing difficulties arising from mental illness. However, there is a large community of individuals who show their mental health battle scars to the world, proving that none of us are alone.

You can find advocates online. They're everywhere. Personally, I love YouTube. I find YouTubers who suffer from mental health conditions comforting. You get to see people's ups and downs and their day-to-day fight. When I was in my worst state, I would binge-watch these types of videos, and it helped me to accept myself. I empathised with the people in the videos and I finally found a social group that I could relate to. Finding people to relate to in life is invaluable, so I thank all of the YouTubers whose channels I watched at that time for supporting me.

Mental health advocates have also increased the level of understanding and empathy that people have for those dealing with psychological problems. As a result, stigma is on the decline, and people are beginning to realise that mental health disorders can be just as severe and damaging as other medical disorders, such as diabetes or cancer. Most people today realise that depression isn't simply feeling sad. They realise that it is a serious condition that affects our energy, our thinking capacity and ability to function for long periods of time. There have been a lot of improvements, but there is still much more work to be done.

People's understanding of bipolar is still particularly hazy. This is likely because it is more complex than other illnesses such as anxiety disorders and unipolar depression. Within this chapter, we will be exposing some of the myths and presenting the facts in a way that will hopefully create a deeper understanding of this illness.

Myth 1: People who are emotionally unstable have bipolar disorder.

*Example: "My boyfriend is really happy one minute, really sad the next and then, all of a sudden, he's angry! His emotions are so changeable all the time. He's been like this for years. I think he is bipolar!"*

Fact: Bipolar is a mood disorder, not a disorder of emotions. It is categorised by long periods of highs, called manic (or hypomanic) episodes and long periods of lows, called depressive episodes. There are also periods of euthymia, where an individual's mood is stable. In this state, individuals are able to function and behave similarly to those without the disorder. There can also be mixed mood states in which people experience both mania and depression at the same time. In this state, a person's emotions can seem very changeable. However, none of these types of episodes lasts forever. In some, episodes may last a couple of weeks, and, in others, they may last for a few months.

In order to really understand why this myth is wrong, it's important to recognise the differences between moods and emotions. Moods are long in duration, and they lower the threshold needed to trigger certain emotions. For example, if we are in a high mood or a manic state, we may be more likely to experience the emotions of happiness, anger, or excitement. If in a low mood, or depression, we will be more likely to experience emotions of sadness, shame or guilt. Emotions are short in duration, lasting a few seconds or minutes, and emotions are easily experienced if the individual's current mood matches those emotions.

Essentially, moods are like locations, whereas emotions are like the people that you will see at those locations. Whether you are in a library or in a nightclub, the people around you will come and go. However, the types of people that will come and go in a library will likely be very different from the types of people that will come and go in a nightclub. In a library, most of the people that you will meet will be working hard and wanting to learn something. In a nightclub, most of the people you will see will be fun-loving and wanting to party. It is possible that the same person who goes to the library will also go to the nightclub, but they will more likely be in one than in the other.

In the same way, if you are in one mood, you will be more likely to experience emotions that are related to that mood. As a result, people who have extreme highs and extreme lows are likely to have intense emotions that relate to those moods. When in a high mood state, we will likely get angrier than the average person or appear to be happier than the average person. In a period of depression, we are more likely to be sadder than most people. This is probably where the misconception that bipolar is a disorder of emotion comes from. The emotions experienced can be heightened.

Our diagnosis of bipolar doesn't mean that we are emotionally unstable. The emotions experienced in bipolar disorder are understandable given the mood state that we are in at the time. If people find the right medications and strategies to balance their moods, then individuals with bipolar will experience moods in the normal realm, and hence will experience emotions in the normal realm.

Myth 2: All bipolar disorders are the same. Everyone experiences them similarly.

*Example: "You can't have bipolar; you've never been hospitalised. To be diagnosed with bipolar disorder, you need to have episodes of mania and episodes of depression. You haven't had mania so you can't have bipolar."*

Fact: There are a number of different possible diagnoses within the category of bipolar disorders. The primary two types are bipolar 1 and bipolar 2. Bipolar 1 is arguably the most severe. To be diagnosed, an individual would need to have experienced at least one episode of full-blown mania, lasting at least one week. Mania is an elevated mood state that is so extreme that it can lead to serious harm to the individual or to others. Consequently, individuals experiencing this state are often hospitalised.

Individuals with bipolar 2 don't experience full-blown mania. Instead, they experience a less extreme version of mania called hypomania. Individuals in this type of episode often appear to be highly productive and enjoy the process of this state. However, as we will see in the next myth, this state isn't as appealing as it may look at first glance.

There are also individual differences in the experience of bipolar disorder. My illness is unique to me. Even if you have bipolar, there will likely be some experiences written within this book that you won't relate to. Although we have an illness in common, our experience of that illness is unique to us. We may find comfort in finding people who are somewhat similar to us within the spectrum of bipolar disorders. For this reason, I use quotes from numerous people who have bipolar to give a range of perspectives and experiences.

Myth 3: Mania is a state to aspire to. It's productive and enjoyable.

> *Example: "I miss being manic. I want to be manic again!"*

Fact: Hypomania and especially mania are not states that one should aspire to be in. There is a reason why mania often leads to hospitalisation. Our mood becomes so high that the irritability, impulsivity and delusions can lead us to harm ourselves or others. Hypomania is often not as dreamlike and awesome as people think either. Pure euphoric hypomanias are incredibly uncommon. Hypomania can often begin as an enjoyable process with high levels of productivity; however, this is short-lived. Generally, the deeper into an episode we go, the more destructive the episode becomes. Despite a lot of energy, the lack of sleep starts taking a toll and the high energy that used to transfer into happiness and pleasure is now manifest as irritability, (Jamison, 2015). Ability to function is damaged socially and occupationally due to irritability and inconsistency; scattered thoughts often lead others to feel confused and bewildered.

If this is the case, why do we often want to be in a manic state? In order to understand the answer to this question, we need to look at the neurochemistry of bipolar disorder. Bipolar leads to imbalances in a number of different neurotransmitters, including serotonin, noradrenaline and dopamine. These neurotransmitters influence our mood, energy and sense of reward. Here, we will only be discussing the role of one neurotransmitter, dopamine. In manic episodes, dopamine levels are too high in certain areas of the brain and this leads to increased pleasure and a feeling of being rewarded, (Ashok et al., 2017).

What else leads to high levels of dopamine? Cocaine and methamphetamine. A lot of people compare mania and hypomania to these stimulant drugs. These drugs increase an individual's pleasure and make them feel euphoric. But there are reasons why these drugs aren't legal. Let's give the example of a cocaine addict called Terry.

When Terry first started taking cocaine, he felt on top of the world, like he could conquer anything. But over time, with persistent abuse of the drug, he developed problems with sleep, he lost his job, and his irritable behaviour cost him his relationship. He then started to believe things that weren't real and sometimes heard voices.

He decided to go cold turkey. But, then, there was a comedown. He fell into a deep depression; one he'd never been in before. The depression, over time, managed to lift, but it wasn't over yet. Even though Terry could see the damaging effect that the drug was having on him, the memories at the forefront of his mind were the best times that he had when he first started taking the drug. He became addicted, and this started a cycle of abuse of cocaine.

We don't willingly inject or snort hypomania or mania. We are unfortunate that our brains have developed a disorder where these episodes invade our lives and cause similar effects to these harmful illicit drugs. Hypomania or mania can trick us in the same way that cocaine or meth can. They can trick us into wanting to go into that mental state again. Part of the struggle of winning the war against bipolar disorder is learning not to be tempted by hypomania or mania.

It's a difficult fight. I myself have come off my medication in the past because I wanted to experience a manic state again. Once I was taught to compare mania to stimulant drugs, I decided to vow to fight mania with all I have. Now, I'm more proactive in my attempts to avoid mania than I am in my attempts to avoid depression.

Myth 4: Bipolar prevents you from living a normal life forever

*Example: "My doctor said bipolar is a severe mental illness and that I need to be medicated for life. I'll never live a normal life."*

Fact: Although there is no cure for bipolar disorder, it can be managed. Millions of people worldwide have battled against bipolar, sought treatment and come out of the other side stronger than before the illness took them over. I know this is true of myself personally. Even before I had bipolar, I never thought I could achieve the goals that I am achieving today. Getting to a stage where we can manage bipolar disorder is like jumping over a massive hurdle. Once we've trained hard enough to jump over that first one, we can jump over any hurdle that life throws at us.

Kay Jamison is just one example of famous individuals who have fought against bipolar and come out of the other side happy and successful. Simply writing into Google: 'examples of people who have overcome bipolar' leads to a plethora of articles, showcasing numerous celebrities who have managed bipolar. Many of these celebrities speak out about their difficult journeys and share some of the strategies they have used to overcome the hurdle. Medication may be something that we need to take for the rest of our lives. But it doesn't mean that we can't live a normal, happy life.

Myth 5: Bipolar medication takes away your creativity and talent.

> *Example: "I cannot be on meds and make watch the throne level or dark fantasy level music."*
>
> *Kanye West on Twitter*

Fact: When we first start taking medication, the side effects can indeed be unpleasant, including the potential to negatively affect our creativity. But, when we find medications that work for us personally and have been consistently taking them long enough for the side effects to dissipate, our creativity can grow to be better than ever. Some bipolar medications, such as quetiapine, have been shown in previous research to improve cognitive functioning, verbal reasoning, fluency and long-term memory, (Akdede et al., 2005).

It took me a long time to find the right medication. For four years, my psychiatrists tried a number of different options and combinations, but nothing seemed to work. At some points, I thought I should give up. The drugs were slowing my thinking, and I found it hard to enjoy creative activities that I would normally flourish in.

Even when I found my current medication combination, it wasn't perfect at the start. My stomach would hurt and my head felt fuzzy. However, within a few months, I realised that it was the longest I hadn't experienced an episode in years and the side effects dissipated. My creative flow was stronger than ever and I started on my journey to become the man I am today. I feel I'm now better equipped to make use of my talents than I ever was prior to taking medication. It took a long time to get here and it certainly wasn't an easy road. But, with good communication and rapport with my psychiatrist, I was able to find the right combination for me, and I couldn't be gladder that I embarked on that journey.

Does Kanye West still believe that bipolar medication is bad for creatives to take? In May of 2019, Kanye West would speak publicly about what he had learnt in the two years following his tweet that bipolar medication is bad for his creativity. Here is the quote:

> *"If you don't take medication every day to keep you at a certain state, you have a potential to ramp up and it can take you to a point where you can even end up in the hospital. And you start acting erratic, as TMZ would put it... When you're in this state, you're hyper-paranoid about everything... Everything's a conspiracy. You feel the government is putting chips in your head. You feel you're being recorded. You feel all these things."*
>
> *Kanye West on David Letterman 2019*

Kanye West realised that the damaging effects of not taking his medication were more substantial than the positive effects. Many thousands of people around the world have achieved huge success while on psychiatric medication.

I hope that this myth-busting chapter has helped you see through the misconceptions that surround bipolar by gaining a deeper understanding of what the disorder is really like. Within the coming chapters, we will be delving into each of the types of episodes and describing, through personal experience and the experience of others, how each of those episodes manifests.

# CHAPTER IV

## *Mania and Hypomania: Part 1: People pay a lot of money to feel the way I do. But should they?*

My grandma was famous for her quick one-liners. She was the type of person who could walk into any room and own it. Her manner was adored by everyone and her wit will always be remembered. One quote of hers that always stays fresh in my mind is "People pay a lot of money to feel the way I do". This phrase is something that I related a lot to in manic and hypomanic episodes and I've used this phrase many times during the course of my illness.

A perfect illustration of what hypomania may look like is showcased in the film 'Limitless'. In this film, the protagonist takes a pill which makes everything in his life enhanced. Everything appears bright and clear, he moves faster than everyone, he thinks faster and is incredibly productive. When I was hypomanic, I watched this film and related to it so much. I'd watch tributes of it on YouTube and dance around in my room thinking about all the awesome and incredible things I'm going to do.

I loved this aspect of hypomania. I wasn't alone in this thinking. Many of us with bipolar can relate to the quote:

> "Who would not want an illness that has among its symptoms elevated and expansive mood, inflated self-esteem, abundance of energy, less need for sleep, intensified sexuality, and — most germane to our argument here — "sharpened and unusually creative thinking" and "increased productivity"?"

Kay Jamison, from the book 'Touched with Fire'

There are aspects of hypomania and mania that are very fun. I've got some crazy and enjoyable memories during those times. I received a lot of attention from women. My confidence and energy levels were so high that I didn't need to try, I was just approached. I loved the attention. Growing up, I felt too shy to talk to girls; I was bullied in school, so suddenly being the person that all the 'popular' guys felt jealous of was really fun.

Despite all the possible positives that can come from hypomania, I would never want to go back into an episode. The negative consequences of doing so are so profound that any positives encountered are made moot. I feel the quote below perfectly describes how episodes can progress:

## Mania and Hypomania

*'There is a particular kind of pain, elation, loneliness, and terror involved in this kind of madness. When you're high, it's tremendous... But, somewhere, this changes. The fast ideas are far too fast, and there are far too many; overwhelming confusion replaces clarity. Memory goes. Humor and absorption on friends' faces are replaced by fear and concern. Everything previously moving with the grain is now against — you are irritable, angry, frightened, uncontrollable, and enmeshed totally in the blackest caves of the mind. You never knew those caves were there. It will never end, for madness carves its own reality.'*

*Kay Redfield Jamison, An Unquiet Mind: A Memoir of Moods and Madness*

Although the beginning of manic or hypomanic states can be epic, episodes of illness can get very bad very fast. And they do more often than not. We can go through periods where we are highly productive, but then something stops us from progressing. Perhaps we can keep up the workload, but our work seems nonsensical to others. Or maybe we become too irritable to carry on doing what we need to do.

Mania is painful. We realise this at the time. The problem is, we forget. We only remember the good parts because, as Kay Jamison said, we develop memory problems towards the end of episodes. For this reason, it's important to keep a journal, so that we can use it for future reference to fully remember and understand our own illness.

One thing that a lot of us who have experienced manic episodes can relate to is writing, particularly writing that involves rhyming. The racing thoughts constantly buzzing around inside our head find connections between everything, be it words or phrases, concepts or objects. This state of mind can really help the flow of words. Here's an example of a rap from a film about a couple with bipolar:

*They call me Luna. Because my mind moves in tune with the lunar shifts. They call me a lunatic… because my biological clock's a time bomb that ticks down to the minute the full moon's lit. And I just got out of the loony bin, and I haven't been taking my medication, so I'm about as unstable as if nitro raped glycerine. More insane than Batman's Riddler if Jim Carrey had played him without taking his Ritalin. I'll leave you riddles sicker than a crossword puzzle written by Jack The Ripper. Full of clues as to how I'm gonna kill you which I will do right before you figure it out so I can stick it on the ground next to your dead body and let the detectives finish filling it out!*

Marco from the film 'Touched with Fire' 2015

## Mania and Hypomania

I love this rap. I think it's fantastic and it paints a good picture of what a manic episode can be like. Things get so ramped up that we feel unstable, potentially a danger to ourselves or others. It's enjoyable, but painful at the same time.

A lot of us can relate to writing passages, maybe poems, raps or prose. I've written all three, however, I particularly enjoyed writing raps. My best friend pointed out something that's incredibly embarrassing. When I rap, it sounds like I'm literally just reading out the words. If you're listening to this on audible right now, that's probably what I sounded like while I tried to rap. I genuinely thought I was amazing at it when I was manic or hypomanic. I also thought I was great at singing, even though I struggle to hit a single note right. That blind level of confidence made me a laughingstock to others. I didn't mind at the time; my confidence was too high to care what others thought. But, in depression especially, and even now, I cringe deeply at those moments.

Often, it takes a while to accept that hypomania and mania aren't things we should strive for. But, after a number of episodes, we often hit a stage where we're done with mania. We realise that the damaging effects far outweigh the positives. When we come to this epiphany, we will do anything to prevent ourselves from going back into a manic state. For me, it took three hypomanic and two manic episodes to get to that point. I fully understand why people often feel like they want to be manic, especially while in the pits of depression. I've been there. But what I realise now is that true stability is far better than any episode. I now feel as productive as I was in any hypomanic episode, without the excess energy. I believe in you to get to the same point too. The quote below describes the mentality I have now:

*I have a chemical imbalance that, in its most extreme state, will lead me to a mental hospital... I outlasted my problems. I am mentally ill. I can say that. I am not ashamed of that. I survived that, I'm still surviving it, but bring it on.*

*Carrie Fisher on PrimeTime 2000*

Once we accept our illness, we can start taking steps in the right direction to improve. If you have bipolar, I believe you can take that step, and I hope that this book can be enlightening in your journey to recovery.

## Part 2 – The Symptoms of mania: my own experience

The latest edition of the Diagnostic and Statistical Manual for Mental Disorders (the DSM-V) is the main tool that psychiatrists use in 2020 to diagnose psychological disorders. In this sub-chapter, we will be discussing each of the symptoms of bipolar, using myself as an example of how this illness manifests in real life. Hopefully, this will give a good indication of what to expect from manic and hypomanic episodes.

The symptoms listed under the category of hypomania are the same as those for mania. The difference between the two is the severity of the symptoms and the minimum duration of the episode. To meet criteria for a manic episode, the symptoms need to last a minimum of one week and need to be severe enough to cause significant impairment in social and occupational functioning. This can often lead to hospitalisation as manic episodes pose a threat to the safety of the sufferer and those around them. In the case of a hypomanic episode, symptoms need to last a minimum of four days. They don't cause enough impairment to lead to severe issues in functioning and they don't require hospitalisation.

So, essentially, if we are so hyper and energised that it's impossible to work, if we're having severely strained relationships, and if our behaviour is risky enough that it could harm ourselves or others, this would fit under the category of mania. If we're energised but are still, at least somewhat, able to function, then we're more likely experiencing hypomania. Here is each symptom and my own experience of each:

*Abnormally elevated, expansive or irritable mood and abnormally increased energy all day every day*

When we're manic, or hypomanic, we have high amounts of energy. Extremely high amounts. During a hypomanic episode, I was with my ex-girlfriend, Emma, and some of her friends. We were going to the park for a few drinks and a picnic as it was a sunny day. It was supposed to be quite a chilled-out event, but 'chilled' wasn't something that I particularly understood at the time. While walking to the park, I kept running away from the group towards tall buildings due to an overpowering urge to climb them. My wall climbing skills aren't the best, so this was mostly to no avail. I didn't mind failing, I just felt so excited and energetic that I felt like I needed to release all that energy. I would run back to the group and put my two cents into whatever they were talking about.

When we got to the park, I was very excited as I was suddenly surrounded by trees. There aren't many things that are more fun to climb than trees. Sometimes, again, I fell because my attempts were rather ambitious. Emma's friends looked at me strangely as if something was wrong with me, whereas Emma laughed and smiled and called me cute. If we're manic or hypomanic, everyone notices that we have abnormally high energy levels. Some like it, whereas others don't.

Another effect of a high energy state is irritability. This can have a negative effect on relationships. Irritability in bipolar disorder is like a volcano inside of us, ready to erupt at all times. We try our best to put a lid on it and stop it from erupting. However, how beneficial would it be to put a lid on a volcano? If someone presses us, challenges us and says something to put us on edge, the lid comes off, and all the lava spills out. It's not just words, it's in our body language too.

I have scared many people because of how angry I can get in an episode. I always feel really bad afterwards, I generally cry and apologise profusely. I don't like getting angry; I hate it. But I'm proud of myself for holding that lid on tight for the majority of episodes. I would often be excited when I was home alone because it was an opportunity to scream and shout and beat my pillow. As a result, I'd feel slightly calmer when my parents got home. It made it far less likely that they'd have to experience my anger. Bipolar rage is horrible for those around us, but it's horrible for us too. My advice is to seek help rather than focus on the guilt and shame over this. We deserve to not have to always feel we have to put a lid on our pain and agony. We deserve to live a normal life.

*Decreased need for sleep*

*"'He sleeps only one hour a night. He's a great man."*
*Tyler Durden from the film 'Fight Club' 1999*

The protagonist from Fight Club certainly does not suffer from bipolar disorder. However, there is an element of similarity between Tyler Durden's behaviour and mania. The protagonist only sleeps one hour a night, and somehow accomplishes a whole lot despite this. Perhaps it's in a very destructive way, but what he accomplishes is still impressive. In my first manic episode, I needed very little sleep to be able to function. I would sleep between one and three hours a night, and some nights, I wouldn't sleep at all. I loved it, at the start, at least.

This was because, even if I couldn't sleep, I somehow had more energy than everyone around. I had more confidence than ever, my skin looked healthier, and I was stronger in the gym than I ever was prior to the episode. In the gym, my bench press was 100kg for two reps prior to the episode. Within a couple of weeks, I was able to do 120kg for three reps. To put that into perspective, that's something that would normally take at bare minimum six months of consistent work to pull off. Add having no sleep the night before I hit those numbers, that's unbelievable.

However, over time, the lack of sleep started to get to me. I went from being amazed that I couldn't sleep to being tearful every night, wishing I could sleep. I started abusing alcohol purely so that I would be knocked out for a few hours each night. A happy, expansive mood state transformed into an irritable and painful one. Delusions kicked in. I believed things that weren't true, causing pain to myself and those around me. I attribute the majority of the severity of my episodes at later stages to my inability to sleep.

I don't say this purely from experience. The link between sleep and bipolar disorder has been shown in research to be a chicken and egg phenomenon, (Harvey, 2008). Poor sleep habits are not only a symptom of mania. They can also trigger manic and hypomanic episodes. Poor sleep habits within an episode can make us more ill, causing hypomania to develop into full-blown mania, or worse yet, a mixed state. We will delve into mixed states in a later chapter.

Medication for bipolar disorder is an important part of the treatment process. I can attribute the majority of my success to my current medications and their ability in giving me a good, rested night's sleep, almost every night. Sleep makes me less likely to go into an episode and less likely to feel irritable. It also helps me to notice the triggers and early symptoms of an episode before things get too bad. This allows me to proactively take steps to prevent relapse.

*More talkative/ pressured speech*

The first symptom that others often notice when we are in an episode is how fast we speak. I'm an introvert, so I don't normally talk that much. I also have a bit of a speech impediment. I stumble on words and sound like an old, bumbling professor sometimes. Perhaps it's a good thing that I'm going into the world of academia where that is accepted. When I'm manic or hypomanic, words are coming out so fast that it's hard for people to catch on to what I'm saying. If I'm messaging someone, I write six paragraphs in the time that they take to respond with a single sentence. Sadly, it's alienated people from me, as some find it overbearing. Others though find it endearing. Regardless of the response of those around us, they will notice a marked difference.

*Flight of ideas and racing thoughts*

*"You know how it feels to have a song stuck in your head? Racing thoughts is like having many songs stuck up there from completely different genres. It's a coming together and an amalgamation of many disparate things. Free-association and wordplay are common – but it's very difficult to focus on just one thing."*

George Dee

As you can imagine, the symptoms of pressured speech and racing thoughts combine to become an interesting and confusing concoction. As I said under the talkativeness symptom, many people have found it hard to keep up with my train of thought. At the time, I didn't understand why they couldn't understand me. It was frustrating. In hindsight, I realise why that was. Not only was I talking fast, but the flight of ideas that were waltzing through my mind led me to change topics too frequently. As a consequence, what I was saying seemed nonsensical.

Racing thoughts can be painful. Imagine a hundred songs stuck in your head at the same time. The level of noise in my head has reached such extreme levels in the past that I felt my brain would explode.

This feeds into the irritability. It's one of the factors that make both hypomania and mania painful.

*Distractibility*

Another consequence of so much energy and racing thoughts is distractibility. At my most manic state, I couldn't read, I couldn't write, I couldn't even watch TV. If I tried to watch TV, within five minutes, I would get distracted, get up and bounce around the rest of the house for the next few minutes or hours. Once I was done with running around the house, going wherever my flight of thoughts took me, I sometimes would go back to my TV programme for another five minutes. Thank God pausing the TV was already a thing by that point. It was rare for me to finish anything I started as a result of this.

*Inflated self-esteem or grandiosity*

We all want high confidence in life. Low self-esteem is a pandemic, and I'm sure that if there was a pill that could make people confident, most would take it. This is likely the aspect of mania and hypomania that is appealing to people. Our confidence goes through the roof and people start to notice. However, there is confidence, overconfidence, and then there's grandiosity.

You have probably heard of people in manic episodes believing that they are the Messiah, or they are going to cure cancer tomorrow. Maybe you have even experienced an episode like that yourself. I've definitely had my own grandiose moments which I realise now are rather ridiculous. Here's a list of mine: I was going to head the biggest business enterprise in China, even though I'm not Chinese. I was going to be the biggest rapper in Detroit, even though I can't rap. I was going to run around the world, including through the Sahara Desert, with just a tent on my back and make international news doing so.

I'm a highly ambitious person, and I like to aim high, but I thought these goals were possible to achieve within days. I am able to laugh now at the ridiculousness of these delusions as plenty of time has passed. But having grandiose delusions and then realising that we're not as capable as we once thought is debilitating. For months, I would think that I was as incredible as incredible can be, and then for the next few months, I literally thought of myself as the worst being on the planet. Depression hits hard after a manic episode, and the dramatic fall in self-esteem is enough to make anyone feel suicidal.

*Increase in goal-directed activity*

Sometimes in hypomania, we feel like a superhero. In some ways, we can even behave like one. We are not telepathic; we can't move things using our minds, and we can't shoot fireballs out of our hands. I've tried to do all of these things when hypomanic, to no avail. But, what we can do is work and work and work all day every day at double the rate most are able to achieve. It's not just a grandiose perception that we have of ourselves either. Others around notice and comment on it. I've experienced some people get jealous that I have sometimes accomplished vast amounts in a very short space of time. There are aspects of this that I love, and the benefits are mostly seen at the start of episodes. However, there are a number of ways that this goal-directed activity can be more of a hindrance than an asset.

Firstly, there is the burnout. The burnout is painful and leads to problems with functioning, extreme irritability and often, individuals then fall into a depression. For long periods of time, nothing is accomplished. Depressive episodes are also generally longer than manic and hypomanic episodes. On average, individuals with both bipolar 1 and bipolar 2 are depressed three times as much as they are manic, (Kupka et al., 2007). For me, episodes of highs lasted approximately three months, and depressive episodes lasted approximately six.

Secondly, the goals strived for in a hypomanic or manic episode can be entirely different to goals that we care about outside of episode. For example, in a few episodes, I wanted to become a self-employed businessman and in one case I tried to become a famous rapper. Outside of episodes, I don't aspire to be involved in business, and I certainly don't care about being a rapper. Sometimes, an episode can be damaging because it takes us on a side tangent in our lives. Regrettably, I've lost jobs due to these 'so-called' productive side tangents.

Thirdly, the level of goal-directed activity has the potential to harm us. During one hypomanic episode, I became obsessed with running. Running was a great escapism for me, and it was positive for my physical and mental health in many ways. I was very fit, and I could run for hours at a time. People would call me Forest Gump as I would just run, run and keep running. My ex-girlfriend, Charlotte, would often shout 'run Forest run", and it spurred me on.

Every time I ran, I would picture Mo Farah straight in front of me. Mo Farah is the Olympian who had, at that time, just won two gold medals, one in the 5000m and one in the 10000m. I would then sprint at the end of my run and picture myself overtaking him. I wanted to get gold in the following Olympics in 2016, and I was determined to train as hard as I could. There was nothing wrong with this level of ambition, and I was very good at running at the time.

At the most extreme points of my training, I would train six hours a day, every day. At the same time, I would barely sleep – perhaps three hours a night. I also wouldn't stretch properly or rest my body. Why? Because I believed I was indestructible. I truly believed, no matter how much I ran, nothing bad could happen to me.

I went on a family holiday to Kefalonia, a Greek island, with my sister Laura and our parents. There was a heatwave, and sometimes, the temperature was in the high thirties in the midday sun. I loved the hot weather. However, I am of Polish origin and I'm very pale with a high propensity to suffer from heatstroke. I would run up and down a small mountain daily in the midday heat. I feel so sorry for my Mum. She was so worried about me. I didn't understand. I thought she was being dramatic. But I now realise that this level of dedication to my goal was destructive. I'm very lucky that I never passed out.

Soon after getting back to the UK, I sustained an injury from overtraining. I couldn't walk. I needed to use crutches at all times for a couple of weeks. I was distraught as I was training for two half marathons which I had organised for twenty-six of us to do a charity fundraiser for my sister Laura, who had cancer. We were raising money for Leukaemia and Lymphoma Research. These runs meant so much to me because I was planning them out of love for my sister. I felt so agitated and irritable, and on the day of the first run, I felt there was no other option. I ran the race. A better description is that I hobbled it. By the seventh mile, runners were stopping their own races, coming up to me and saying that they'll take me to an ambulance. That's how bad I looked. I was crying, but I kept telling them "No!". I needed to run this. I pictured my sister in my mind and channelled all my rage and anger into this run. I finished the race, which is quite epic considering that I couldn't walk the day before. However, the consequences simply weren't worth it.

My injury became so severe as a result of this decision that I will never be able to run properly again. I've lost one of my greatest pleasures. Although goal-directed activity in manic and hypomanic states can feel awesome and, in many ways, seems impressive, by becoming so excessively fixated and overzealous, we have the potential of getting ourselves in dangerous situations.

*Risky behaviour*

The risky behaviour in manic and hypomanic episodes are heavily linked to what has already been discussed. The level of overconfidence in these high mood states can lead people to believe they are invulnerable to danger. Although running is a healthy activity, the level of overconfidence I had at the time led me to train in very risky ways.

With all the risky behaviours that I've engaged in during manic and hypomanic episodes, I am lucky that I am still alive. You know that you're very ill when a man who spent years in prison calls you the craziest person he's ever met. I found it funny at first, but now, as I look back, it's sad and alarming. The effect of the mania is not only on the person experiencing it but also on those who care for them the most. I regret that my mania has hurt those I love.

I'm going to relate a story of something I did when manic that still haunts me to this day. It wasn't at all intentional, but it still can bring me to tears even now. My Dad organised a holiday for my sister as a celebration as she had just recovered from leukaemia. I was ecstatic about this as I love my sister Laura very much. But, the day before this holiday, I did something I feel is unforgivable.

My ex-girlfriend, Charlotte, messaged me at 11 pm and invited me to join her at a house party. I wasn't going to sleep that night anyway, so I thought to myself, what harm can be done by going. She told me that they were running out of alcohol so I should bring some with me. Thinking I was meant to buy enough for everyone, I turned up with a litre of amaretto and a litre of rum. She scowled at me when I arrived, asking why I brought so much. She wanted me to bring just enough for myself.

Another guest challenged me to a drinking competition. I laughed, thinking this guy had no chance against me. I was so confident that no matter how much I drank, nothing bad could happen to me. I thought that I'd be fine for the flight the next morning. I was downing the amaretto straight from the bottle. People found it highly entertaining. Charlotte… not so much. She tried to stop me, but nothing could prevent me from attempting to down both bottles. By the time I finished the amaretto, I had started on the rum, and this is where my memory fades completely.

I woke up the next day in the hospital with a drip in me. As I opened my eyes, my Dad was understandably angry and said we had missed the flight. I looked at the time and saw it was three hours until the flight was due to take off. I immediately said that we could still make it. I truly thought I was fine even though there was a drip in me, and I had drunk an excessive amount of alcohol without any mixers. I got up, drip still connected, threw up into a bowl and passed out again.

My Dad had to rearrange the flight, and it cost my family a couple of days of the holiday. I was very lucky that they decided to stay with me while I was ill. I didn't deserve it. I'm so sorry to my whole family for this and for other horrible things I've done. Laura, and all of my sisters, are incredibly important to me. Laura is eight years older, has looked after me and has loved me since the moment I was born. I don't want to hurt anyone, especially those that I love. If there is one regret I have, it's that I didn't try harder with medication and relapse prevention earlier. Part of it was due to the inadequate care I had from mental health professionals at the start of my illness, but I truly believe I could have done more to help myself.

However, I don't beat myself up for the errors I have made. I was so mentally ill that I didn't realise that there would be consequences for my actions. And when the consequences came, I was surprised yet didn't learn from the experience. I viewed it as a fluke and went back to believing I was indestructible.

This is an aspect of the grandiose delusions experienced within mania. I hope, if you don't suffer from bipolar disorder, you can read this and realise that that the loved one you care about or the patient you see isn't doing these things because they feel like taking a risk. They aren't doing these things because they want to hurt you. Their brain is preventing them from seeing the true consequences of their decisions.

## Mania and Hypomania

*Not due to drugs, medication, other treatment, or other disorder.*

As mentioned earlier, cocaine or meth can have similar effects on the brain and on behaviour as manic episodes. Also, prescribed medications can sometimes have strange side effects that can lead people to similar behaviours. For this reason, it is important for any psychiatrist to ask and assess whether their clients have been taking drugs or medications that could explain these symptoms.

Likewise, it is important to see whether these behaviours could be due to another disorder. For example, individuals with schizoaffective disorder can experience manic states. It is also possible that some manic-like behaviour could be due to a psychotic episode. For this reason, it's important for any psychiatrist to take a personal history from either the patient or from a relative or friend if the client is too ill.

*Unspoken symptoms*

I've experienced all the symptoms listed in the diagnostic criteria that have been mentioned in this chapter. However, there are other symptoms that I, and many others with bipolar, often show within manic episodes. One that appears to be very common is paranoia and paranoia-related-psychosis. Not everyone that experiences it has a similar story to me; however, I want to share mine.

At one point during mania, I came up with the spectacular idea of planning strategies that would lead to world peace. You know, the typical Monday morning routine. I was spending time every day, dancing in my room listening to songs that made me feel powerful. This included Eminem, Linkin Park and Kanye West. I felt like the songs were speaking to me, giving me vital information on how to solve all the problems in the world: poverty, inequality, crime and abuse. The more I listened to music, the more confident I became in my plans.

However, then, an obstacle appeared. An insane, psychopathic clown was trying his hardest to destroy all my efforts. He loved the chaos and hated all the work I was doing. The Clown became my enemy. He's 'The Clown' with a capital T and a capital C because he was the villain in the story, and I was the hero. The relationship between myself and The Clown reminded me somewhat of Batman and The Joker, complete opposites and sworn enemies. My name was Zedman, a superhero that I created as a child based on my sister, Zosia, as I looked up to her immensely whilst growing up.

Sometimes, I would visually see this Clown as a hallucination, and, at other times, I would hear him.

The Clown permeated my relationships. I was convinced that The Clown was trying to turn people against me, be it loved ones or complete strangers. I was scared. I felt defeated. I felt like this Clown was preventing me from doing what I felt I needed to do. I felt anxious to leave the house as I believed that the Clown would try and attack me through other people. I felt helpless, and I felt alone, as I knew nobody would believe me.

This is just one example of how psychosis and paranoid thinking can affect individuals in bipolar mania. Regardless of how it affects, it's scary and can have severe negative consequences. These symptoms are often seen in depression too and are particularly common in mixed states. However, in depression, the paranoia is often related to low self-esteem rather than a supervillain stopping our heroic ventures. In depression, I have become paranoid that other people view me as weak.

# CHAPTER V
## *The Symptoms of Depression: My own experience*

*"Depression is not just 'feeling sad'. It's physical too; there's this huge weight on you, draining you of energy and making your body sore. You use sleep to escape. And then you just don't want to wake up again because the weight of it all takes you under."*

George Dee

As humans, we all go through dark periods in our lives where we feel there is no escape; the sadness takes over with a dark cloak, blinding us from seeing any light. For most people, these low points are triggered by something tragic happening in their lives, like the loss of a loved one or the break-up of a relationship. I'm glad that the modern mental health movement is creating a world which is more accepting of these common forms of psychological discomfort.

Major depression is far more severe than simply feeling down. It's as if we become zombies, devoid of all positive emotion. Each night, we feel exhausted after fighting another day that we wish we didn't need to. Each morning, we wake up and wish we hadn't. Sadly, a quarter of our population will experience a depressive episode within their lifetime. Some research suggests that this is the case for approximately 30% of women and 20 % of men, (Kruijshaar, 2005).

At my deepest, darkest point, I had no confidence. I don't use the term 'no confidence' lightly here. There was no activity that I felt confident enough to do. I felt that, if I washed the dishes, I would drop the bowls or cups and break them. They wouldn't be clean enough, and I would fail to put them in the appropriate cupboards afterwards. I had the same problem with the dishwasher. I love eating eggs, but I had no confidence to even hold them in my hands, let alone crack them. I was sure I would drop them and then I wouldn't know what to do when the egg was on the floor. I believed that there was no activity that I was skilled enough to complete. This is an example of how anxiety and depression feed into each other. Like the perfect partners in crime, they plot and conspire against us, robbing us of our spirit, leeching our very zest for life.

I felt sad sometimes. There were bouts of tears, but mostly, there were feelings of emptiness. It was like I was at the bottom of a deep pit, so dark that blackness was the only thing I could see. I didn't exist. Nothing in my life had any purpose, and I was unable to find pleasure in anything. Video games, movies, and music did nothing for me. I just wished I could sleep and sleep and sleep. I would try and sleep the majority of the day and would just stay in bed most of the time doing nothing. I got a slight sense of pleasure from eating sugary foods. Because I didn't care about my own health at that time, I would eat excessive amounts of Cherry Bakewells, which are small tarts with white icing and a sugary cherry on top. I would eat packets and packets of these. I didn't care about the possibility of developing diabetes. In this respect and, in fact, in every respect, it's the exact opposite of mania. In mania, I wouldn't realise the consequences of my actions. If I did realise them, I would have cared profoundly. In depression, I knew the consequences, but I didn't care at all. When we have no self-worth, we feel like there's no point in anything.

I experienced suicidal ideation most of the time, and it got to a stage that was unbearable. I decided I wanted to hang myself in my room. As I was to have the house to myself for the entire day, it seemed an appropriate time to attempt it. I had almost finished setting up the preparations when, fortunately, my Mum came home. She wasn't feeling very well, so she decided to cancel her plans last minute. My Mum came up to my room to find out how I was. She knocked on the door. Panic-stricken, I opened it slightly, leaving it ajar, eye-poking through the gap. She asked whether she could come in. I said "No". She looked rather concerned and asked why I wouldn't let her in. I decided to make a joke out of it. I told her "You know me, I like being suspicious", with a cheeky smile on my face. My Mum and I always joked together, so she didn't question me further, laughed and left. After seeing her beautiful smile, I chose life. I cried quietly to myself. This was a turning point.

I started to feel better. My mood lifted slightly, and I could gain some pleasure from video games again. I took small steps to try and regain my confidence. I started to load the dishwasher. Slowly but surely, I was able to fill it up. Perhaps it took four attempts. Then came trying to make scrambled eggs. I tried my best, but the worst thing possible happened. I dropped an egg on the floor. I felt so shaken by this and so unsure what to do. I stopped trying again for a bit; it was too difficult. A week or so went by, and I started making small steps again. Slowly, my confidence began to come back, and, within a few months, I was able to do necessary activities such as make food and wash the dishes. I was still a long way from being confident, but steps were being made in the right direction.

*Very little interest and pleasure in anything*

*"If all your favourite hobbies were colours, depression is a horrible dark beast that not only causes you to be colour-blind but also leads you to forget what colour looks like."*

When we are depressed, it feels like all light has disappeared. Everything we once loved becomes a drag. Having conversations with friends or relatives often ends with us feeling more down than we felt before. Yet, being in isolation leaves us feeling even worse. We can't win. Perhaps the worst aspect is that we forget what pleasure even is. The only memories we have are dark and miserable. This is what makes depression so debilitating. There seems to be no light at the end of the tunnel. This can be especially pronounced if the depressive episode follows a manic or hypomanic one; an utter sense of disillusionment settles inside us, where all our previous plans and projects that filled us with excitement before, are suddenly emptied of any meaning, pleasure, or joy.

*Psychomotor agitation or retardation/ loss of appetite or eating often*

Everyone experiences depression a bit differently. Some people can't stop moving their leg, others struggle to move at all. Some feel they can't eat; others eat all the time. Personally, I find it hard to move, and I eat constantly. This isn't the best combination as I'm prone to having a bit of a beer belly.

## Fatigue or loss of energy

We feel exhausted constantly. Doing anything is strength-sapping. This is why I often think of bipolar as a disorder of energy. We have high energy states and then low energy states. Both are equally extreme and equally difficult to manage. With no energy, we feel like we don't exist and everything, including time, is moving so slowly that time appears to stand still.

## Feelings of guilt and shame

We feel that we don't do anything right, and so everything is our fault. We may apologise profusely to people for minor errors such as forgetting to turn off the heating or dropping a plate on the floor. Although some evidence suggests that guilt is a relatively healthy and adaptive emotion, the extent to which it is experienced within depression is weighty and hard to bear.

Shame is like guilt's evil twin. Guilt is a feeling of responsibility or remorse for a real or imagined offence. Shame is where we hide away from something that makes us feel humiliated. For example, instead of apologising for dropping a plate, we may hide and not confess it was us.

Shame has been described in the past as 'the swampland of the soul', (Brown, (2011, October).

Each time we avoid memories which we view as shameful, the swampland grows. As the swamp becomes more deep, dark and dreary, our need to hide from it increases. We do this because we find it hard to trudge through the thick mud. Avoiding those shameful memories feels like a good idea. However, a horrible feeling grows, and the water becomes stagnant. We begin to sink, and the pain gets harder and harder to deal with. In contrast, when we experience guilt, we are able to get over some of the feelings as we express them outwardly. This is what separates it from shame; we trap ourselves in the swamp's quicksand, allowing it to take full control over us because we feel we don't deserve any better. In Section 3, 'Be Your Own Psychologist', we will discuss the topic of shame further and how to process it.

We have been discussing the shame and guilt in major depression. The experience in bipolar depression is even more extreme. It's not because bipolar depression is a heightened version of major depression. It's because of what we likely had just experienced prior to the depressive episode. If we have a manic episode followed by depression, we suddenly see the truths that we were previously blind to. We see the mistakes we made when manic or hypomanic and feel profound grief for the people we might have hurt. The 'me in the depressive episode' finds it hard to understand the 'me that was manic', and as a consequence, we blame ourselves entirely.

I've felt excessive amounts of guilt, and particularly shame during depression. It's painful, and until we walk through that swampland and try to overcome it, the pain will always be there.

*Can't concentrate and indecisive*
Even if we found the motivation and confidence to engage in a task, it's very difficult to concentrate. Reading a book, as I've said previously, was a struggle. To read a single page and digest it was difficult. By the end of a paragraph, I would forget what I had just read and have to re-read it. No matter how much time I would spend on a single page, it would be very difficult for me to fully grasp what it was trying to tell me. This fed into my already low self-esteem. Whenever I did try hard to engage in tasks, my problems with concentration made me feel even more defeated and unworthy.

Due to a lack of confidence, we also experience severe indecisiveness. This leads to paralysis, with nothing being accomplished. We don't know how to make a decision, let alone start working on it.

*Recurrent thoughts of death and suicide*
Often, we believe that we'd be better off dead. The lack of pleasure in our day to day lives and the ab-

sence of memories of positive experiences from the past, lead us to believe that our future will be nothing but misery. When people try to tell us 'there's light at the end of the tunnel', it frustrates us because we feel nobody understands. We feel like nothing has ever gone right in our lives. If someone tells us that we have been happy before or shows us a picture of us with a smile on our face, we believe it is simply proof that we are good at masking the pain. We are sure that we have never experienced pleasure, and every time people have perceived us as experiencing pleasure, we have succeeded in deceiving them.

Thoughts of suicide come often. Sometimes, it's as simple as I wish I was dead. At other times, we may contemplate methods of action. Sometimes, we even come up with a definite plan. Some people experience this level of suicidality and choose not to go through with it. This was true in my case. I think the reason I have done this in the past is that I like knowing there is a way out if I need it. Battling with bipolar at times can feel like we are forced into a war where we have no room to manoeuvre. By having suicide as an option, I guess I felt more in control. I felt that being in this war was my choice. By not choosing suicide, I felt that I had decided to fight, which gave me the ability to continue.

## The Symptoms of Depression

Sometimes, people do make an attempt. Some choose methods that are highly likely to result in death, and sadly, many lives are lost. Some individuals may harm themselves in ways that could potentially kill them but are unlikely to. This is sometimes viewed as a cry for help, but I don't think it's quite that simple. Sometimes, we may feel like our emotions are so intense that we feel a need to release them in a physical way. This would explain why people engage in self-harm behaviours that are unlikely to kill them and yet are very painful.

Suicide may seem like the only option at the time, but our lives are far from over. I never thought I'd be able to do anything with my life, and yet, now I'm proud of all of my achievements. Once any of us balance ourselves in the right way, a way that I will try my best to show you in this book, then we can become stable and genuinely enjoy our lives. If you or someone you love are suicidal right now, I'm very sorry to hear that. I'm giving you a big bear hug. I hope that my words in this book can give you some hope, but please seek help from professionals. I believe in you to get through.

# CHAPTER VI
## Mixed episodes and rapid cycling – How am I going to survive this one?

### Part 1 – Mixed Episodes

*"Mixed episodes are truly the worst. If depression is a blue shirt and mania a pair of red trousers, then a mixed episode is the utter mess when both are chucked in a violently shaking washing machine that could explode at any moment."*

George Dee

Mixed episodes aren't as common as mania or depression, but if you've ever had a mixed episode, you know what I mean when I say that it is truly unbearable. A mixed state is when you meet all the criteria for mania and all the criteria for depression at the same time. In these episodes, I felt like a human oxymoron. I couldn't stop moving, and my brain kept firing. But, at the same time, I had no confidence in myself. The irritability was intense. This, combined with the inability to see any hope in the future, left me feeling suicidal. I felt like the options were to kill myself or to hurt others. It took a whole lot of self-restraint to stop me from getting physical in any confrontations that I had at the time. I was scared for myself, scared for others, and I felt so much guilt and shame for the times when I couldn't keep a lid on my volcano of irritability.

I decided to go to the hospital as I wanted to section myself during one of my mixed episodes. I was scared that the anger would get so severe that I could seriously hurt someone. My family were there with me, being incredibly supportive throughout the process. The hospital didn't have enough beds at the time, a common problem in London, UK. They said that because I have a supportive family around me and that I seem like a 'nice boy', I should return home with my family. I was seriously concerned for my own safety and others', so this distressed me deeply. I have to admit, though – my family are fantastic, and I've been very blessed to have people around me who have been supportive. Without that support, I truly don't know what I would have done. However, if someone goes into a hospital and says that they are worried that they may seriously hurt someone, the staff should section them. Imagine if I didn't have enough self-restraint and someone was seriously harmed.

When in the midst of a mixed episode, seeing a good psychiatrist is the best route. I know my psychiatrist has helped me find the ideal medication regimen that gives me a good night's sleep. This can aid in the reduction of my episode's severity and length. Medication isn't going to get rid of the episode completely, but it can help in lessening its impact long term and prevent the likelihood of an episode arising again in the future.

## Part 2 – Rapid Cycling

Rapid cycling can occur in either bipolar 1 or bipolar 2. This term is used when an individual has a minimum of four separate mood episodes in any given year. They must switch to an episode of the opposite polarity each time. For example, an individual may have a hypomanic episode in January, a depressive episode in March, a manic episode in July and a depressive episode in November. I have experienced rapid cycling for two years.

This is very destabilising. The good thing about bipolar is that we can get periods of euthymia where functioning is normal, and we feel stable. In rapid cycling, it feels like that stability is never there, making life a lot harder. Going through rapid cycling can have damaging effects on our cognition long term. I've noticed this to be the case in my own life.

Imagine being on a rollercoaster that is consistently going up and down with no periods of rest and that this continues for a long time. When we finally get off the rollercoaster, we still feel disoriented. We have become so used to the ride that we feel sick, we can't think straight, and our vision is blurred. This is what euthymic periods feel like following rapid cycling. Even though the episodes have ended, we still feel the effects on our cognition and functioning.

# CHAPTER VII
## *What have we learnt here?*

Within this section, we have broken down the different types of episodes within bipolar disorder and discussed how they manifest. We have differentiated between bipolar 1 and bipolar 2 and have explained that each individual has a unique experience. Having an in-depth understanding of bipolar disorder is important for two main reasons. Firstly, we realise that we aren't alone. Approximately 2% of the population has a bipolar disorder, (Merikangas, 2007). That may sound like a small percentage, but it means that millions of people worldwide experience this condition.

Furthermore, understanding bipolar is the first step in helping us to identify if we or someone we care about is currently in a mood episode or seems to be entering one. It was only when I gained a comprehensive understanding of bipolar disorder that I was able to notice my triggers and prevent myself from going into an episode. Finally, understanding bipolar helps us to realise how severe this disorder can become. At the start of the disorder, we some-

## What have we learnt here?

times enjoy mania. I hope this section has convinced the reader of the importance of relapse prevention and consistency in taking medication.

We will now look at how we can use therapy to our advantage. Section 2 discusses how I learnt to spot a good therapist, all the mistakes I have made in the therapy room and how I learnt to make the best of my therapy.

# Section 2:
# How to make the best of therapy

# CHAPTER VIII
## *Why doesn't therapy work for me?*

If you were to ask ten people who have attended therapy for their thoughts on their experience, you'd likely get a wide variety of responses. Some will say that attending therapy was the best decision of their lives. Others will say that it was pointless. Some will say that they experienced some benefits at the start and then these diminished, whereas others will say that the therapy left them feeling even worse than when they started. How can a form of treatment have such a large range of responses? Are some people untreatable?

I thought I was untreatable. I believed this for a long time. Years of going to see different therapists with very little benefit, caused me to question my therapists, the mental health system and myself. A bitterness grew within me. I saw no hope. What's the point of trying if it's to no avail? I'm glad I persisted. In recent years, I have attended two courses of therapy which have helped me greatly. I attribute a lot of my current success and happiness to both treatments, and I'm eternally grateful to both psychologists who had a significant impact on my life.

There are a number of factors that affect the quality of therapy. Each of these will be discussed in this section. Using a combination of personal experience, the experience of friends or clients, and documented research, I will be sharing the main factors that influence whether a therapy will be useful or not. I hope my own experience can help whoever is reading this, be it someone with mental health difficulties, a therapist, or a loved one, to understand how the benefits of therapy can be enhanced. As cognitive behavioural therapy (CBT) is currently the primary form of therapy for bipolar, we will be discussing most of this from a CBT perspective. However, I believe the same principles can be applied to any form of therapy.

# CHAPTER IX
## *Go for the right reasons*

We've already compared the relationship between a therapist and their client to the relationship between a tutor and a pupil. No matter how talented a tutor is, their pupil won't be successful unless they take the active effort to engage in the sessions. The student needs to have the desire to adapt and improve their strategies within the subject area. A pupil's grade on an exam doesn't automatically improve due to the talent of their tutor. It takes an active learner to apply that wisdom and use it to improve their own performance.

Likewise, regardless of the talent of a therapist, we will not benefit from therapy unless we actively work alongside them. As with a tutor, we go to the therapist with problems that we are struggling with. These problems are within us. They are the situations, thoughts, feelings and behaviours that we are having difficulty with. The therapist teaches us concepts and strategies that may help us with these problems. It's our job to test these strategies and see whether we reap some benefits.

*Go for the right reasons*

This process isn't easy. It takes a considerable amount of motivation to complete internal work successfully. We are often working against beliefs that we have held for our whole lives or strongly entrenched patterns of behaviour. As a result, we need to go into therapy for the right reasons. The only motivation strong enough to fully benefit from therapy is to be convinced that this will help us. We need to want to get better. We need to want to live a more fulfilling life.

I initially attended therapy because my mum wanted me to. I'm glad that I went, as it alleviated some of my mother's distress. However, as I went for the wrong reason, the therapy did not benefit me. I wish I had tried harder in the therapy room and had realised its importance at this stage. Nevertheless, with failure comes knowledge, and the knowledge that I learnt from these failures has taught me a lot.

We can't force ourselves to want to get better. This is something that comes naturally with time. However, I came to realise two things about therapy that helped me in this regard. Firstly, I decided that therapy isn't about changing who I am; it's about giving me strategies to live a more fulfilling life. People often say, 'you need to want to change'. When we hear this, we shy away from therapy.

Change is a scary word. Over time, I developed the goal to discover the real me, to focus on my strengths and to live as meaningful a life as possible. It's as if I stopped viewing therapy as a place where I should change, to a place that helps me see myself as I really am. I think viewing it in that way helped me.

Secondly, we need to believe that it is possible to improve. We need to have hope. Even a tiny sliver of hope is enough, if we hold on to it tightly. Sometimes, it's scary to hope. We're all scared of being let down, especially by ourselves. I gave up many times, thinking I'd never feel better. Now I'm one of the millions of people worldwide who have done what they thought was impossible. I've worked through my problems and am now able to enjoy my life. I believe everyone deserves and is capable of this.

# CHAPTER X
## Rapport:
## *It's not just about 'getting on' with your therapist*

Therapeutic rapport is essential in the development of a healthy therapist-client relationship, (Leach, 2005). The client needs to feel safe, respected and able to open up fully within the therapy room for any tangible progress to be made. To build a good level of rapport takes effort from both the therapist and the client. The therapist needs to be approachable and to show high levels of empathy and understanding to the client. In turn, the relationship must be reciprocal, and the client must also show respect, empathy and understanding towards the therapist. One of the most important components of building a good relationship between client and therapist is establishing a safe space in which the client is able to be honest and one where they feel unjudged.

When there is a good therapeutic rapport, the client will feel safe to discuss things that they find difficult in their lives. They feel comfortable enough to embrace a vulnerable state in the therapy room and fully let the therapist come into their world. In my experience, there were three factors that differentiated a good rapport from a bad one.

## 1) To all therapists – please listen to us

Some therapists fail to listen to what we're saying. To truly listen, a therapist needs to devote their full attention to hearing the account from the client's perspective. Some therapists I've met have been overly opinionated, appear to wait for their chance to speak and tell me things about myself that I don't necessarily agree with. The therapist may have good intentions in this strategy, but its consequences outweigh the benefits due to the cost it has on the therapeutic relationship.

Perhaps one reason why therapists can be outspoken within the therapy room is that they want to provide structure. Structure is important, and psychologists are taught to use psychological theories to support the clients in their own progression. However, viewing the therapy room as a space to tell the client answers to their problems isn't healthy. Socratic questioning is a far better approach in providing structure to the process.

A number of clinical psychologists have taught me that the subtle art of being a therapist is to listen attentively and then provide guided questions for the client to make their own decisions, (Kazantzis et al., 2014). This is better for the client's own development, and it also builds a strong rapport between them. In order to be a great teacher of any subject, the teacher needs to truly listen to the student in order to understand them and their goals. They can then use leading questions to create a structure that guides the pupil to meet those goals. For example: Why do you think this is the case? Are there any reasons to doubt the evidence? What led you to that belief? These are all examples of Socratic questions that can provide structure to the therapy room. This is a CBT principle; however, the same reasoning can be applied to any form of therapy.

*2) Feeling awkward or shy around the therapist*

Even if our therapist is great at their job, there are times that a strong therapeutic rapport is never built. Some people just don't gel. I have met many people in my life with whom I find it hard to converse, and you probably have too. Sometimes, talking to certain people is laborious. It's hard to open up to them and form a good relationship. Personality differences count for a lot in any relationship.

Sometimes, the therapeutic rapport can't be formed because something makes us shy about talking to that therapist. Some individuals find it hard to open up to men. Others may find it hard to open up to women. I've struggled to open up to men for most of my life. This is likely because the male role models I've had, despite being wonderful people, have not been emotionally open people themselves.

Although I find it easier to open up to women, there were somewhere that wasn't the case. As an eighteen-year-old boy, it wasn't very smart of me to see a thirty-year-old female psychologist whom I found to be very attractive. I wasn't able to be open with her because I felt shy in her company and wanted her to think well of me. The therapy room is one of the most vulnerable places we can be in, so we need to make sure the person is someone we feel comfortable enough to build a healthy and honest relationship with.

*3) Allowing ourselves to feel vulnerable*

As clients, we need to try our best to aid the process of creating a healthy therapeutic rapport. I think the biggest thing that holds a lot of individuals back is having issues with expressing vulnerability. I wanted to be a robot, free from any vulnerabilities or insecurities. I wanted to be like a Vulcan from Star Trek, purely logical and not letting any feelings sway my decisions. I viewed this as strength and something to strive for. This mentality prevented me from making healthy progress.

One of the most famous researchers on the topic of vulnerability is Brené Brown. She has a TED talk on the power of vulnerability which I would recommend to anyone reading this book. Simply go on YouTube and search 'Brené Brown power of vulnerability', and you will find her speech. In our modern era, we are taught that vulnerability is a weakness and that we should hide from it. Growing up, Brené Brown was a believer in this philosophy. She was brought up with the mentality that it is weak to be vulnerable. She wanted to study vulnerability and was certain she would find that it had a profound negative effect on our lives.

She was taken aback when her findings revealed the exact opposite. Her research indicated that a lot of problems in modern life begin with failures in embracing vulnerability. Apparently, this caused her to enter a mini breakdown. Her whole philosophy of life was questioned by her own findings. As a woman of science, she carried on research within this area, despite the research contradicting her personal views. Delving further into the topic, she found that failings to embrace vulnerability left individuals with both the inability to fully experience positive emotions and the inability to process and work through negative ones. Her perspective changed, and she now strongly advocates for people to embrace their vulnerabilities.

If you are struggling with expressing and accepting vulnerability as part of who you are, then I strongly recommend doing some soul-searching and watching some of the work of Brené Brown. Embracing vulnerability is one of the most vital steps to therapy as, without any expression of vulnerability, the therapeutic rapport is impossible to form.

That being said, a fantastic therapist can sometimes help an individual to get past that hurdle and feel vulnerable. I know that I only benefited from therapy when I'd already embraced my vulnerabilities. Within Section 3, we will delve deeper into this topic.

In summary, to create a good therapeutic rapport, our therapist needs to truly listen and ask thought-provoking questions. We need to choose a therapist whom we feel comfortable opening up with. We also need to accept that the therapy room is a safe space and embrace our vulnerabilities with open arms. If our therapists and us follow these three steps, a great therapeutic rapport will follow.

# CHAPTER XI

*Don't go when in the midst of an episode: Especially not a manic one!*

There is a reason why most psychologists believe it's best to begin therapy during periods of euthymia. When we're stable, we are more self-aware, more motivated for positive change and are, for the most part, cognitively able. Both manic and depressive episodes can dramatically reduce the amount of benefit gained from therapy.

Why isn't therapy useful when we're manic? When we're manic, we often don't want to come back to reality. This is especially the case in hypomanic episodes. We tend to enjoy the highs and revel in the amount of excitement, passion, and drive that's oozing out of us. Although we notice that there are aspects of mania that we hate, we can deceive ourselves by viewing the therapy room as a place where we can learn to reduce the 'negative' symptoms of mania, whilst maintaining the level of excitement and drive.

Secondly, people in a manic state experience a lot of magical thinking or delusions. When manic, people often believe things which aren't realistic. For example, they may believe that they are the Messiah or that, if they research and read as many books as they can tonight, they can come up with the cure for cancer tomorrow. Even if our experience of magical thinking isn't as profound as this, in a manic or hypomanic episode, our thinking isn't clear or realistic. This means that, if the therapist is discussing an aspect of our cognition that could be holding us back, we're unlikely to actually take it in and use this information.

Thirdly, being manic causes gaps in our concentration and memory. Even if we want to concentrate and take on the advice that our therapist is giving us, it's difficult to absorb the information and apply it to our lives. Racing thoughts lead us to be highly distracted. To get the most out of therapy, we need to stay alert and on task. In my personal experience, being manic in the therapy room has led to little being accomplished, as I change topics too frequently.

Earlier in this book, I mentioned a female therapist that I was attracted to. We will use the example of my sessions with her to explain how therapy, when experiencing mania, can go wrong:

I had so much energy at the time that I would be bouncing in my seat at the start of each therapy session. Although at that time, I enjoyed the majority of the emotions that hypomania brought me, it was all too much. I had too much energy, and this caused me to be agitated, to struggle to sleep and feel in pain. I wanted to reduce these symptoms, which is why I proactively wanted to engage in therapy.

I viewed each therapy session as a short-term fix for my bipolar symptoms. She would use the technique of progressive muscle relaxation to help me calm down. This is a form of meditation where an individual is guided to tense and then release each muscle group, one at a time, from the head to the toes. Progressive muscle relaxation is useful for everyone, even for those without a mental health diagnosis. I highly recommend looking for a guided progressive muscle relaxation recording on YouTube or elsewhere. This meditation helped me short term in the therapy room and also helped me to have a better night's sleep.

However, the benefits were short-lived. The next day, I'd be back to bouncing around, attempting to climb trees and houses. Because I was viewing therapy as a short-term fix, I was only getting short-term benefits. We get out what we put into whatever we do. When manic, we often like aspects of our illness. As a result, our behaviour stays the same.

I also wasn't cognitively ready for therapy. In order to fully benefit, we need to have the ability to look at things objectively and apply the words of wisdom directed at us. At the time, running was my biggest passion, and I told my therapist that I had a goal to run around the world with nothing but a tent on my back; to run all day every day and pitch my tent to sleep at night. I really thought this was an achievable goal and even thought that running through the Sahara Desert was realistic. I wasn't daunted by the blistering heat or lack of water. I truly was blind to the fact that I could be endangered by things around me and was deluded into thinking that nothing bad could possibly happen to me.

Due to all the reasons described in this chapter, she decided to terminate our therapy at the end of ten sessions. She's the only therapist who'd ever told me that they wished to stop having sessions with me. You'd think that I'd be saddened by this and that I would feel rejected, but I was too manic to care. I just smiled and waved to her and then started bouncing around again.

-

It's also not a good idea to begin therapy when we are depressed. When depressed, we lack motivation and struggle to see the light at the end of the tunnel. Even if we manage to come to important and ground-breaking conclusions about our cognition, we don't realise the full importance of it due to our own negative thinking. We become fixated on the past. We believe, when depressed, that there is no hope in our future. Anything that can help us long term will go in one ear and out the other.

Although I have read this in research, I also know this from personal experience. I have been attended therapy when depressed. Sessions became a source of comfort, helping me to survive one week to the next. There was some benefit. It helped me survive the episode. I viewed it as a space where I could offload my emotions. Therapy, and especially a practical form of therapy such as CBT, should focus on the future and how we can work on things now for a better tomorrow; how we can use psychological theories to start on the road to recovery. This is virtually impossible when depressed. This is why it's best to attend therapy during euthymic periods.

# CHAPTER XII
## *What is the therapy about?*

Imagine attending a maths class, not even knowing what maths is. The most intelligent person on the planet could enter an A-Level maths class, but if they don't know that numbers can be added, subtracted, divided, or multiplied, the whole class would be complete gobbledygook to them. In order to learn any subject, we need to begin by understanding the base principles that make up that subject. The same reasoning applies to therapy. We need to understand the underlying principles that make up the form of therapy before we can start reaping the benefits.

Perhaps I've watched too many films, but I always viewed therapy as a place where you lay on a couch, tissue box in arm's reach, talking about your mother and recounting all the upsets that took place in your childhood. I pictured a stern, bearded man with legs crossed, jotting notes down and nodding along throughout. I didn't realise at the time that this was, for the most part, an obsolete stereotype. Contemporary therapies are much more structured,

## What is the therapy about?

not just a safe space to talk through past experiences. Talking therapies are somewhat similar to the general notion many of us have when we think of the word 'therapy'. It can be very useful to have someone with whom we can feel safe to talk. Being confident that what you're saying is being listened to by the therapist is important. However, this perception of therapy is considerably different from practical based therapies, such as CBT. Going into CBT with this perception of therapy would be like going into a maths class, knowing only how to count. Essential to maths, but there's a whole lot more to maths than just knowing how to count. It's only one aspect of a very complex subject.

When I first attended CBT, I was determined to do my best to make sure the therapy worked. I plonked myself on the couch and decided to go against every compulsion within me and talk about my childhood and all my feelings. I was so proud of myself, as this sort of soul-bearing was incredibly difficult for me. And yet, here I was, opening my heart to a complete stranger. The therapist tried to use Socratic questioning, worksheets or CBT principles to bring some structure to the therapy. I listened but would go back to talking about my childhood. It's as if when we were discussing one plus one is two, I didn't realise my therapist was actually attempting to make me add numbers, rather than just repeating the numbers out loud.

CBT is a practical, goal-oriented psychotherapy that aims to help clients to see how their thoughts, behaviours, and emotions all interact and feed into each other. It aims to show us that the ways we respond to situations in our lives can be adjusted so we can meet our goals and reduce our symptoms. In order to know where we're going, we need to know where we've been. This process involves some aspects of discussing the past, as this is the springboard to our journey. However, it mostly revolves around discussing thought-behaviour patterns that we have in the present. We then test or decide whether these thoughts and behaviours are damaging to us. Following this, we can develop strategies to modify aspects of these thoughts and behaviours. This can help us to reduce our symptoms and get closer to our goals. If I had known the purpose of this therapy, I would have made better use of it.

Good communication is key to laying the foundations of a therapeutic relationship. The therapist should be able to provide clear, comprehensive answers to any of the patient's questions relating to the therapy's method and goals. This should be established from the very first session. The more knowledgeable we become, the more beneficial the therapy can be. My most recent CBT was the most bene-

## What is the therapy about?

ficial because I had experienced the therapy before and had been taught about it when studying psychology. The more control and autonomy we gain over our own psychoeducation, the better our therapy experience will be.

These principles can be applied to any form of therapy, not just CBT. The main goal of any therapy is to end the set of sessions as our own psychologist. We want to use the principles within the therapy in our own lives and manage our illness better. Approaching life from this perspective is the fundamental reason why I'm able to finally say that I enjoy life.

# CHAPTER XIII
## *Do the homework*

When a child comes home from school, the last thing they want to think about is homework. They will procrastinate as much as possible. They may play some video games or chat with some friends. In the end, for the most part, they do it. This is generally because of the immediate negative consequences that will come their way if they don't. Maybe their parents will ground them, or maybe they'll get detention at school, or worse yet, both. The immediate negative consequences of not doing their homework are strong enough to induce them to do it – at least most of the time.

It's hard to motivate ourselves to do our therapy homework as there aren't any immediate negative consequences of not doing so. The therapist may look disappointed for a brief moment, but they will quickly get back to the day's topic. In order to be motivated to do homework, we need to not only envision the long-term positive effects but also be inspired by them.

## Do the homework

I have struggled with wanting to do homework. Sometimes I wouldn't do it at all, or at other times, I'd complete it but leave it at home. It wasn't just laziness. At the time, I struggled to get any structure in my day, and my organisation was poor. Having bipolar for a number of years and many episodes within that period caused severe levels of dysfunction, even in euthymic periods. I believe that, if I had realised the benefit of the homework, I would have been able to complete it and bring it in despite these limitations.

Homework is a major component of CBT. The reasons for this are many. Some homework is active in nature, asking us to practice things learnt within the sessions and applying them in our lives. Then, we go back to therapy and discuss how it went. Sometimes, it goes very well. At other times, we may struggle to apply things learnt in therapy. If things work out smoothly, then we can establish new behavioural patterns immediately, which can improve our lives. If, however, we aren't as successful from the outset, we can still benefit from the process. Struggling with this type of homework may reveal other underlying issues that can then be worked on further within therapy so that the next time, we may be more successful.

Secondly, it teaches us that we are capable of working on improving ourselves without the support of the therapist. Just as a tutor can't take the exams for a student, the therapist can't always be there to guide us throughout life. We need to learn how to proactively work on our own mental health. We are generally more able than we previously believed and can surprise ourselves with how well we do in our homework.

Thirdly, only so much can be achieved in a one-hour session. Homework allows much more to be accomplished each week and makes each session more meaningful, as the previous homework can be discussed and worked upon. Studies have reliably shown that clients who complete their homework gain more from therapy, and the reasons that we have just discussed are only a few of the many benefits, (Rees et al., 2005).

There are many different types of homework in CBT. Some of them will be discussed in Section 3. For now, we will just look at three major categories that most CBT homework assignments fall into: psychoeducational, taking action, and monitoring. We will discuss each of these three types of homework in turn.

*Psychoeducational homework* is where we are given leaflets and worksheets that explain concepts and theories within the model. For example, in our first session, we may be given a CBT model info sheet. This worksheet will help us to understand the pur-

## Do the homework

pose of CBT and why we are doing it. As mentioned in the previous chapter, understanding CBT is vital in getting the most out of therapy, so paying attention to this early homework, that may seem easy and pointless, is incredibly important. Psychoeducation also improves adherence rates as people realise the severity of what they are facing, that it's a real problem and that treatment options can work if approached correctly.

Another key component of the homework assignments is *taking action*; taking what has been taught within the sessions and applying it to real life. For example, I have told a therapist that I often think 'I'm not good enough' when I see that there are dishes that need to be loaded in the dishwasher. This thinking used to lead me to avoid using the dishwasher at all, as I was scared that I would get it wrong and prove that my belief of my incompetence was correct. If I did load the dishwasher, my anxiety would lead to the physiological response of persistent shaking. This shaking sometimes led to me dropping cups or bowls on the ground, further validating the thought that I wasn't good enough.

To get rid of this negative thought-behaviour interaction, my therapist told me to counteract that voice and say 'I am good enough' three times. Over time, the voice saying I'm not good enough began to diminish, and I felt more able to achieve the task.

This small change in my behaviour led to the first step of what is now a dramatic change in my ability to function. Homework is part of the reason why I'm now able to study and do well in my life.

The third type of homework is *monitoring*. The therapist may ask us to monitor the events or feelings that are experienced during the week. The two that stood out the most to me were tracking moods and tracking daily activities. Sometimes, I would forget how I felt each day the week before. By tracking moods, we can monitor whether we are likely to relapse and whether any improvements can be seen due to certain strategies being implemented. This is informative and provides us with clues on the next steps that we should take.

Documenting the activities that I engaged in throughout the week was particularly useful to me. The first week, I was shocked by how little I actually accomplished. This inspired me to try each week to slowly increase the number of activities I was engaging in. At the start, I did very little except listening to music all day, eating and showering. My therapist said it's a good start that I was already looking after myself by showering. I slowly started to incorporate new activities into my daily routine. It was difficult, but I know that I wouldn't be where I am today without the incremental steps I was taking at that time.

*Do the homework*

In summary, there are many different types of homework in CBT. I followed it somewhat and didn't think much of it at the time. However, upon reflection, homework was one of the two main components of CBT that has helped me improve my cognition, symptoms and functioning long term. The other was my therapy blueprint.

# CHAPTER XIV
## *Your therapy blueprint is your best friend*

A best friend knows us inside out. They remind us of who we are, how we've progressed, and help us stay on the path to the future we dream of. A best friend never gives up on us and always stays at our side. When we embark on CBT therapy, we leave knowing that we likely will not see the psychologist ever again. But we come out with something incredibly valuable – a best friend.

The main goal of CBT therapy for bipolar is relapse prevention. Bipolar is an episodic illness, so if we know the strategies that can reduce the chance of relapse, we can begin to manage the illness. A therapy blueprint is a CBT tool that summarises the work that a therapist and patient have completed together. The therapy blueprint contains what has been learnt regarding the past, present, and future. I'm holding my therapy blueprint right now as I write this chapter and will be referencing it throughout. I made a little book as my therapy blueprint and made it look quite pretty with big handwriting and nice colours. I'm far from the best artist, but it's good enough for me. I believe that making it appealing has helped me to refer to it often. It's nice to look at and easy to read.

When documenting the past, we go into what the main problems were, how the problems began and what made them recur. The front cover of the book showed some negative thinking patterns I had prior to starting therapy. Growing up, I always wanted to be perfect. I always tried to act like a robot, void of all emotions, so you can imagine that, when bipolar struck me, it was difficult to deal with. I came to a realisation that I wanted to feel the highs because I felt more productive and more powerful. I wrote that if I didn't do things 'well enough', I was very hard on myself. I struggled to accept failure and was heavily prone to guilt and shame. Also, I had the opinion that being on medication made me weak. These thought patterns were ways of thinking that I previously thought of as positive. Over the course of therapy, I realised that these thinking patterns were negative because they were a barrier to recovery.

On the first page on the inside, I wrote about the coping mechanisms that I had prior to therapy: the negative and the positive. I wrote all the negative ones in red, such as alcohol, sweet food and takeaways and all the positive ones in blue, such as therapy, meeting friends, and gym.

Then we documented the present. Within this section, I drew a spider diagram talking about what I had learnt. This included maintaining consistency with my medication, learning that it's okay to experience some emotions and that it's just as important to look after my emotional health as my physical health. I need to be kind to myself and acknowledge my feelings. I wrote that, although I still had a lot to learn, my coping mechanisms had improved, and I felt more of a sense of self. I then wrote my new coping mechanisms, including Tai Chi, writing, gym, running, and making videos for my own YouTube channel.

On the back page, I wrote about how I wanted to become stable. I wanted a future where I could have a family and live a happy life. I wrote that I wanted to become my best self, rather than wanting to be the best. I wrote that I wanted to focus on caring about others rather than always thinking of my own problems.

Of course, this change in thinking patterns and behaviours doesn't fix bipolar disorder. But it helps in improving cognition in ways that prevent a future episode, as we think and behave in ways that support rather than hinder our mental health. Each individual is different, and your therapy blueprint will likely look very different from mine. However, having one acts as our best friend. Mine reminds me

*Your therapy blueprint is your best friend*

who I am, who I was, how I've improved, and what I should strive for next. It is still useful to me, even five years after I made it.

I also wrote a relapse prevention plan which went alongside the blueprint. It contained behaviours that I have since always tried to keep consistently in order to prevent relapse to both mania and depression. I thought I would share this with you:

*Plan for relapse into mania*

- Stay on meds
- Make sure I sleep seven hours each night
- Allow myself to feel more vulnerable rather than wanting to be a robot
- Deal with stress through gym, poetry, music, being social, changing environment
- Reality checks are needed regularly
- Focus on making realistic goals

*Plan for relapse into depression*

- Stay healthy physically through gym and diet
- Make realistic goals and check with others to make sure they are realistic
- Do things that improve my self-esteem: poetry, music, gym and being social

- Remember that the storm will pass
- Work on effectively solving problems
- Work on deconstructing negative thoughts

In the past five years, this list has grown substantially. However, at the time, this was ground-breaking and set me on the right path to continue my recovery journey.

I keep my therapy blueprint and relapse prevention plan in a folder with all the homework and in-therapy-worksheets that I accumulated over my twenty-two sessions of CBT. It's a thick folder with a lot of information. When I go through periods of illness, I can look through it and remember how I managed in the past.

-

In the last few chapters, we have delved into the world of therapy. We've discussed how to make the therapy work, how to use homework to our advantage and how to gain long term benefit from therapy blueprints. Although we have used the example of CBT within this section, these principles can be applied to any form of therapy. I've learnt these principles through my own lived experience and the many mistakes I made. I've also learnt this information from the research and courses that I have undertaken in the past few years.

# CHAPTER XV
## *Why did some of my psychiatrists benefit me and others not?*

I'm not a psychiatrist. I definitely don't have the credentials to tell doctors how to do their job. But I have met some psychiatrists who have impacted my life in a positive way and others who, I feel, made my journey harder than it should have been. Many people with bipolar that I know have mentioned that they've had at least one psychiatrist that did more harm than good. I wanted to give my personal opinion here on what makes some psychiatrists great and others not so great.

Firstly, the psychiatrists that have helped me the most have truly respected and listened to me. They took the time to take a full and expansive history from me about my previous episodes and life experiences and listened to my opinions on my mental health and how treatment should proceed. They have shown care by taking an interest in me as an individual and treating me as a human being rather than simply 'a bipolar patient'.

My first psychiatrist made me feel uncomfortable and never even took a history from me. I was in a mixed episode, and it was my first episode of this kind. He was confused by my mental state, saying that I can't have bipolar as I wasn't strictly in a manic or a depressive episode. Clearly, he hadn't researched bipolar enough to know of mixed states. If he had taken a comprehensive history, it would have become clear that I'd had numerous hypomanic episodes and depressive episodes prior to that point. These are very basic errors that, in my opinion, shouldn't be made by a professional. Sameer, whom I have mentioned previously, a specialist in bipolar disorder, was astonished about this and very unimpressed by the lack of insight in the diagnosis. Sadly, this is quite common. Other people with bipolar have experienced similar situations with at least one psychiatrist.

Secondly, the best psychiatrists I've met take a balanced approach to medication. My second psychiatrist put me on a low dose of a particular antipsychotic. I later found out that, at this low dose, the medication acts primarily as an antihistamine. In other words, it wouldn't be helpful in preventing mania or depression. When I inevitably fell into an episode of mania, my psychiatrist completely changed the treatment approach and decided to put me on a very high dose of a different medication. I

### Why did some of my psychiatrists benefit me and others not?

had stomach pains, was lethargic and fell into a depression. This new medication is known to be useful for mania but isn't particularly helpful for depression. It was only when Sameer helped me to understand the actions of medications better that I realised how ridiculous this treatment approach was.

The best psychiatrists I've met explained the purpose of the action of medications and what bipolar disorder is from a medical standpoint. They drew the mood swings on a piece of paper, showing the episodes like a large wave, indicating long periods of mania and depression. They then showed that the purpose of the medication is to reduce the length of highs and lows, and the severity, so that they become smaller, shorter waves. They told me that it's normal to have ups and downs; the only issue is the extent to which it's experienced in bipolar disorder. They told me that medication should act to have a balance between restricting mania and lifting the mood to prevent depression. It's a fine art. By working with a great psychiatrist, I was able to find that balance.

Again, I am not an expert in psychiatry. I am simply an individual who has bipolar disorder. I have observed some psychiatrists who have helped me and others who haven't. If you're a psychiatrist reading this, I hope that this can show the perspective of a client and can be informative in some way. If you're a patient or a loved one, I hope this can help you to spot a good psychiatrist. Also, the more knowledge we gain about ourselves and our condition, the better our relationship with our psychiatrist can become. It is our responsibility as patients to gain an understanding of exactly what is causing us trouble, and it is the responsibility of a good psychiatrist to explain the disorder and how the medication works in helping us manage it.

# Section 3:
# How to become your own psychologist

# CHAPTER XVI
## *Know your illness, know yourself and know the difference between the two*

So far, we have discussed the importance of learning what bipolar disorder is and how therapy can be used to our advantage. Learning this information gave me the foundation needed to know how to approach the war. Better the devil you know than the devil you don't. Gaining this knowledge helped me to know what I was fighting and the capabilities of the support network surrounding me. Only then could I begin developing the strategies needed to win. To fight back against my enemies and conquer them.

The way we fight back against bipolar is by becoming our own psychologist. Our war is unique to us. We all have different triggers and experiences, and learning how to fight our war is a personal struggle. No one else can fight it for us. Within this section, we'll be discussing what I have learnt on my journey. A lot of this can be applied to any mental health disorder. However, it is particularly applicable to bipolar.

Becoming my own psychologist wasn't easy. It wasn't a quick process. It was one baby step at a time, toddling my way to victory. I fell over often. I may have cried a bit, but I got back up and started again. Slowly, I learnt how to walk stably. A toddle turned into a walk, and a walk turned into a run.

The beginning stages were the most difficult. The first step was to remember who I truly am. Mental illness can be likened to a veil. It blinds us and makes us only see things from the lens of the disorder we have. It distorts the way we see the person in the mirror. Years of persistent ups and downs caused me to only know the 'manic' me and the 'depressed' me. I didn't know the real me anymore. I defined who I was by the label 'bipolar'. In my mind, I 'was' bipolar. I had to find a way to lift the veil. I had to realise that I have bipolar rather than allow the disorder to define who I am.

I thought I knew who I was. I thought I had great self-awareness. But then, I had an epiphany. I was sitting in a therapy room with a fantastic CBT psychologist. He showed me a worksheet which appeared to be rather simple, but it ended up being far more challenging than I would have ever thought. I had to explain on the worksheet what I'm like when manic, when depressed and when I am stable. There was a list of dimensions, including mood, attitude towards the self, self-confidence and preferred activities. The goal of the worksheet was to recall what I am like on each of these dimensions when in an episode and when stable.

Although I found it easy to describe myself when manic or depressed, I couldn't think of a single word to describe who I was when stable. For two years prior to this, I was experiencing rapid cycling. Periods of stability were rare and short in duration. I had become accustomed to the rollercoaster ride that bipolar took me on.

I was a bit worried about the extent to which I was struggling with this worksheet. I always prided myself on my level of self-awareness and maturity regarding my mental health. It was humbling as I grew to realise how early on my road to recovery I was. I recognised how detrimental the perspective 'I am bipolar' was to me. Hence, I used as many techniques that I could to develop a better understanding of myself.

I began to look at childhood photos. I asked my family questions about what I was like prior to developing this illness. I tried to meditate and reflect on all the things that have consistently been important to me throughout my life. All these strategies helped me to develop a better understanding of who I am without bipolar.

Within the coming weeks, I began to fill out the stability column of the worksheet. It was slow, but it

*Know your illness, know yourself and know the difference between the two*

was motivating seeing some progress in this area. Here is the list of dimensions that I was asked to think about. For anyone diagnosed with bipolar, I would strongly suggest jotting these down and trying to fill out what you are like in mania, depression and euthymia. It may be difficult, but with time and reflection, it will come to you. For the first five, I give examples of what I wrote so you know how a therapist would guide you to fill out each section.

*(1) Mood*

When manic, I feel elated and irritable.

When depressed, sometimes I feel nothing at all. At other times, I feel the need to cry. Nothing can give me pleasure.

When stable, I feel passionate and consistent. I have a drive which helps get me out of bed in the morning.

*(2) Attitude towards self*

When manic, I am grandiose.

When depressed, I view myself as worthless.

When stable, I have a positive self-esteem, yet have insecurities, in the same way anyone does. I believe in myself and my capabilities, but sometimes I question myself. I find I struggle most when I feel my intentions aren't as good as I'd like them to be.

*(3) Self-Confidence*

When manic, my self-confidence is through the roof.

When depressed, my self-confidence is non-existent.

When stable, I felt positive about myself and in my abilities. I'm naturally confident. But I'm not confident in social situations or about my physical appearance.

*(4) Usual activities*

When manic, my usual activities are socialising, writing poems or raps, and exercise. I also like taking risks. I tend to become obsessed with one thing, and most of my attention is directed in that area.

When depressed, I play video games and eat junk food.

When stable, I play music, run, go to the gym, and do research on mental health. I often do projects. For example, I have designed magazines and written short stories. I enjoy creative activities.

*(5) Social activity*

When manic, I see friends daily.

When depressed, I go for months without going out to meet friends.

When stable, I see friends every two weeks or each month and am naturally introverted. I'm also quite shy.

Here is the list of the rest of the dimensions on the worksheet I was given:

*(6) Sleep habits*

*(7) Appetite/eating habits*

*(8) Concentration*

*(9) Speed of thought*

*(10) Creativity*

*(11) Interest in having fun*

*(12) Restlessness*

*(13) Sense of humour*

*(14) Energy level*

*(15) How noise affects you*

*(16) Outlook on the future*

*(17) Speech patterns*

*(18) Decision-making ability*

*(19) Concern for others*

*(20) Thoughts about death*

*(21) Ability to function*

Although I already knew a lot about my bipolar disorder, writing about myself during mania and depression helped me spot the warning signs of my illness. This made me better equipped to spot whether I was going into an episode early enough to prevent full relapse. It wasn't too difficult for me to fill out this part of the worksheet.

I'm happy that I began to realise who I truly am. Normally I am passionate and consistent, yet I'd forgotten that my passion and ambition were enduring qualities within me. I had forgotten that I always had high self-esteem before being afflicted by bipolar disorder. I always had insecurities, especially regarding my social abilities, but it never affected me in other areas of life. It just left me rather shy and introverted. This was a healthy level of insecurity which I have finally accepted as part of who I am. I would sometimes be happy and sometimes be sad. I cared about justice and would stand up for what is right.

Remembering who I was before bipolar was a revelation. I always had a balanced view of myself and my life prior to bipolar. Lifting the veil helped me to increase my self-esteem. I realised my talents and remembered what is important to me. We are not bipolar; we have a disorder. When I was small, I was stoic and consistent. If you had asked a teacher whom they thought, within my year group, may develop this mental illness, I'd be near the bottom of the list. Bipolar can happen to anyone; it isn't about personality. Learning whom I was helped me to take steps to feel more like myself again.

In summary, learning what we are like in episode can help us to spot episodes early and respond. Learning what we are like when stable boosts our self-esteem and helps us know when we are healthy. In the next chapter, we will discuss a technique that we can use to improve our self-awareness.

# CHAPTER XVII
## *Journaling*

As a child, when I thought of journaling, I thought of Lisa Simpson with her Dear Diary entries. Journaling seemed to be reserved for gushy talk about high-school sweethearts or awkward loners who struggle with social interaction. Looking at it that way, perhaps I should have spent more of my time journaling. I wasn't the only one who had this view. This was the common conception in the 1990s and 2000s. In the past few years, opinions on journaling have changed dramatically.

Most YouTubers and social media activists in today's age are all about self-care and self-improvement. Journaling is a topic that is frequently brought up and described as an anchor which keeps highly effective people self-aware and moving in the right direction. Many people subscribe to this movement and vow that it is one of the most important additions that they have introduced into their daily routines.

However, if you were to ask ten people how they journal, you'd get a wide variety of responses.

Everyone has a different approach, and the techniques used are entirely down to the individual. There is no rule on how we should journal. However, methods of journaling seem to fall into two main categories: journaling our feelings and journaling to change our outlook.

*Journaling my feelings*

Talking about feelings is something I've always found hard, and it's something I've tended to shy away from over the years. Hence, journaling about my feelings isn't something I regularly did. In hindsight, I wish I had. Research has shown that this form of journaling helps people to manage stress, understand themselves better, solve problems more effectively and have healthier relationships, (Purcell, 2006). This makes journaling useful for everyone and explains why it is so often advocated.

Bipolar is a rollercoaster ride which leads to increased stress and issues with resolving our thoughts and feelings. Also, it often negatively impacts our relationships. As a result, journaling our feelings is particularly important for people with bipolar disorder. George Dee, a good friend of mine, recommended this form of journaling to me. Here is what he says about this activity which he engages in daily:

*"One benefit of this type of journaling is that by tracking our daily mood, we can identify and spot our early warning signs. For example, if you need less sleep than usual, this might be heralding an upcoming manic episode. With this knowledge, we can be better prepared and even halt a mood episode altogether.*

*The second main benefit that I have seen is that it allows us to have a healthy way to externalise our problems. Sometimes our emotions can get so intense and all-encompassing that our imperative need to externalize them may manifest in unhealthy or unproductive ways. On the other hand, sadness, frustration, anxiety, and a large host of other feelings that can accompany bipolar disorder can also have deleterious effects if silenced and bottled up. It is here that journaling can help solve this conundrum, as a journal is not unlike a canvas, granting us unbound freedom to vent and self-express our hopes and fears.*

*Finally, keeping a journal can help us self-reflect and examine our internal thought processes in a similar way to mindfulness-based meditation. By grounding us in the present moment, we are able to feel safe and express our thoughts and feelings, without needing to judge or analyse them. We can then later return to the page and see that we were merely caught in a temporary thinking trap, gaining experience and insight into how our minds can trick us.*

*It is thus easy to understand how valuable a journal can be for our mental health. What is more, there are no stone-set 'rules' that must be followed; you are completely free to choose the method, form, and style of your journal. Whether free-flowing or more structured, it all comes down to what you are most comfortable with."*

*Journaling to create a positive outlook*

For the most part, I journal to improve my outlook, become more positive and achieve more each day. If you haven't noticed so far when reading this book, I like structure, and I like order. I start my journal entry by writing a plan for the day. I write more goals than I am usually able to accomplish in order to make sure I'm as productive as possible. Then, I write three things that I'm grateful for. I may write about something nice that happened to me the previous day, such as a stranger smiling at me or a family member being kind to me. At other times, I write that I'm grateful to have a bed to sleep in each night and a roof over my head. Reminding myself of my many blessings helps me to remember how fortunate I am in the grand scheme of things.

Finding gratitude is difficult at first, especially when we have a mental disorder as severe as bipolar. We've experienced so much pain over our journey that it's hard to fight each day, let alone develop an optimistic outlook. Sometimes, it's hard to think of anything we're grateful for. We're so consumed by the agony we're in that we are blinded to all the good.

Even when we write something down, we don't always feel gratitude. It's as if we are aware that these are things that we should be grateful for, but as the pain outweighs the good, we don't actually feel grateful. With persistence, I managed to develop the ability to feel gratitude. It's like a muscle. We need to train in gratitude daily for long periods of time for the appreciation to be fully experienced.

The positive effects on my life have been profound. I think the biggest change I've noticed has been in my enjoyment of my relationships. I feel much closer to my family, girlfriend, and close friends. It also helps me in relapse prevention. I'm thankful that I developed a grateful attitude as it helps me to avoid depression. It appears to me that the more we are grateful, the harder it is to fall into that mood state, (Lambert et al., 2012).

This is my favourite type of journaling. That being said, always trying to be positive when we're feeling depressed or negative can get us in a pattern of avoidance, which isn't healthy. It's healthy to accept our emotions and work through them, not simply force ourselves to change. This is why it's likely best, if time allows for it, to engage in both of these types of journaling. Only by both writing about how I feel

*Journaling*

and thinking of positive psychology strategies to improve the quality of my life, have I been able to enjoy all the benefits journaling has to offer. It's a fine balance, and finding our own personal balance can help us to develop optimally.

# CHAPTER XVIII
## *Know your triggers*

Awareness of the situations that trigger episodes of mania and depression can help us to avoid environments that negatively impact on our mental health. The more we avoid situations that stress us and put pressure on our mental health, the less likely we will be to relapse. The phrase 'prevention is better than intervention' is common in the field of psychology. Although spotting early warning signs and intervening does work well a lot of the time, preventing us from being triggered is an even better strategy for relapse prevention. If we are able to avoid the situations that trigger us to go in an episode, we are far less likely to relapse. I try my best to choose environments that are unlikely to lead me to become stressed. I choose friendships, holidays, and daily activities which are calming.

That being said, some stressful situations in life are unavoidable. For example, my parents will likely die before I do. However, knowing that we have been through a triggering situation allows us to keep a keener eye on our behaviour. We begin to suspect

*Know your triggers*

that early symptoms are on the horizon and get prepared for what could come next. Then, we can use the tools in the previous two chapters to tell us whether we need to intervene.

Over time, I have learnt that my biggest external triggers for mania are sudden changes in my environment, sudden changes in my diet, a new relationship, a break-up of a relationship or dysfunction in a friendship. For example, recently, I felt triggered that I may relapse into an episode. For four months during lockdown (due to COVID-19), I was living with my girlfriend. It was just the two of us together, and I loved it. I became used to this way of life. However, the time came for her to return to Hong Kong for the summer. I was sad to see her go but excited to move back home from University to my family. I went from an environment in Sussex where everything is green and there are lots of beautiful walks to go on, to the hustle and bustle of London. I also decided to stop being friends with someone who had a severe ego complex and who enjoyed putting me down.

All of these situations were sudden, and they impacted on my life. Recognising these triggers allowed me to become vigilant of my own mental health. I noticed that my mood was elevated, and I was having problems sleeping at night. In response, I started taking a PRN medication (a medication that

I choose to take when needed) that I was prescribed for when I struggle with sleep. My sleep returned to normal. I tried to engage in grounding activities, such as meditation. This helped to calm me. Knowing my triggers here and spotting the early symptoms allowed me to adapt and prevent myself from returning into an episode.

Perceiving myself to have failed in something has often been my main trigger for depression. For example, I had a job in sales, and the CEO was an unscrupulous man taking advantage of his employees through a pyramid scheme. I couldn't stand how he was treating his workers, so, I tried what I could to improve matters. My efforts and achievements in this regard were not appreciated by the CEO. He retaliated and tried his best to make my life as difficult as possible. He succeeded in doing so. I became depressed as a result. This was five years ago now. Likely, if something similar happened now, I would be able to spot the triggers and prevent the episode from occurring, as I did in the previous example. At that time, I wasn't aware enough, and unfortunately, it resulted in the longest bout of depression I've ever had.

Everyone's external triggers are slightly different. It is our responsibility to work out our own triggers so that we can recover. Journaling our feelings should help with this. Journaling can reveal the pat-

*Know your triggers*

terns that occur before episodes begin. Then, we can take steps to prevent an episode.

# CHAPTER XIX
## *Action plans: Know how to respond*

Once we've developed a greater awareness of ourselves, we can start writing up an action plan. A personal action plan is an outline of coping strategies to prevent or limit an episode of bipolar disorder. I have two action plans, one for mania and one for depression. In my own experience, the best action plans have been where I write out (1) the triggers (2) the early symptoms (3) a list of responses I shouldn't do and (4) a list of responses I should do. Although this is particularly useful for episodic illnesses, like bipolar, these principles can be applied to anyone that experiences mental health difficulties.

*(1) The triggers*

I first write out all my potential triggers as well as the steps I can take to avoid them. For example, I know that surprising situations are triggering for me. This is even the case for good surprises, such as a surprise birthday party. I have told my friends and family that I prefer not to be surprised so that they

## Action plans: Know how to respond

know to be direct and upfront, avoiding any out of the blue situations that could potentially startle me. This small change has helped me a lot.

I also write a list of unavoidable situations that are triggering. For example, a family member falling sick is unavoidable. For these types of triggers, I write out the type of episode they often give rise to, so that I know which early symptoms to look out for.

*(2) Early symptoms*

I then write out the symptoms which precede a depressive or manic episode. For mania, I have noted: reduced sleep, a preference for fast-paced music and a constant need to move. For depression, I have written down a numb feeling, sad mood and feeling tired. These tend to be the first symptoms experienced prior to a mood episode.

*(3) List of responses I shouldn't do*

Often when heading into an episode, we do the exact opposite of what we should do. When approaching mania, I couldn't hold my excitement and wanted to stay up all night, listening to music full blast while dancing crazily in my room. Sometimes, I'd also sing my lungs out. I feel sorry for my neighbours as I always keep my windows open. I also liked to watch movies and TV shows and relate to the high functioning but slightly wacky characters.

'Limitless' and 'Legion' were two of the biggest culprits for me in this regard. I also would often choose to make a drastic change in my diet or exercise routine. Although having a good diet plan and exercise regime are beneficial, sudden changes in even positive ways often lead me to develop an episode. This may not be the case for everyone, which is why we all need to write individualised action plans.

In the case of depression, I would often sleep in as much as possible and would refuse to open the blinds until the sun was about to go down. I would gorge on sugary food and junk food and wouldn't engage in any exercise at all. Leaving the house was rare and social activity was avoided.

I think a lot of us get impulses to do the exact opposite of what we should do when we are approaching an episode. It's difficult to stop ourselves from doing exactly what our bodies are commanding us to do. I find it hard even now. Do I always succeed in inhibiting these impulses? No, not even close. But I try and limit them as much as I can. At times, I still love dancing in my room without a care and watching my favourite movies and shows, but I make sure that I go to sleep at a reasonable hour. I have found a balance that works for me.

Action plans: Know how to respond

*(4) List of responses I should do*

I then write the responses I should do instead. For example, when I start noticing I'm becoming hyper, I begin taking my PRN medication to help me sleep. I contact my psychiatrist to alert them that I may be approaching an episode. I do activities that relax me, like Tai Chi and meditation.

For depression, I make sure I socialise a bit, even if I don't feel like it. I contact my psychiatrist and try to leave the house almost every day. I also try my best to accept negative thoughts and then let them pass. When we are watching YouTube, we're sometimes interrupted by those perky ads which take five seconds before we can skip them. This can be frustrating, but we skip the ad and carry on watching our favourite videos. As we go about our days, it's natural for negative thoughts to pop up in our noggin. The target is to get to a stage where we are able to accept those negative thoughts, let them do their thing, and let them go. Intrusive negative thoughts are common. Dwelling on them is where issues can begin. If we can become aware of this bad habit and make this a part of our action plan, we can reduce the likelihood of going into a depressive episode.

Within this chapter, I have discussed my own action plans. Essentially, we should engage in activities that balance our mood — for example, focussing on medication and doing activities that either relax us or make us feel happier. We also avoid activities which may be tempting but risk relapse. By managing to do this, we can enjoy some stability in our lives.

# CHAPTER XX
## *Manage Stress*

Think back to the last set of exams you did. Your school or college likely told you that these exams would influence all your outcomes in life; that success in these exams was vital for you to live the life of your dreams. At least, that's what my school would always tell me. A moderate level of stress is healthy. It motivated me to study and work hard. I felt a boost in efficiency and memory. However, as the days passed and the exam date got closer, I began to get too stressed. My concentration waned, concepts I was trying to learn seemed to go in one ear and out the other, and I started to get angry. Sometimes, I would avoid studying in order to fly away from this stressful feeling. I've noticed that stressful situations like this are the biggest triggers for my episodes.

Stress is something we all experience. It is essential to our survival. Stress is what motivates us to respond to difficult situations by either fighting hard or fleeing. However, intense stress and prolonged stress aren't good for physical or mental health.

Stress has been shown to precede relapse and recurrence of mood episodes in bipolar disorder, (Ellicott, 1990); (Koenders, 2014). As a result, most therapists and workbooks focus on stress management skills. Here, we'll be discussing three strategies I have used to improve in this area.

*1) Exercise and diet*

Studies have reliably shown that frequent exercise is a fantastic way to reduce stress, (Fillingim et al.,1992). Although it's difficult to get started, once we get into the swing of repeated exercise, it can become addictive – in a good way. This is because exercise has effects on our neurochemistry. It reduces stress hormones, such as adrenaline and cortisol and increases levels of endorphins, (Nabkasorn et al., 2006); (Thorén et al., 1990). Endorphins are natural painkillers in the brain, and they act as mood elevators.

What we eat also affects our neurochemistry, (Funston, 2020). Complex carbs, such as oatmeal, stabilise our blood sugar levels and prompt our brain to increase serotonin levels, improving our mood. Foods high in magnesium, such as leafy green vegetables reduce fatigue and stress levels. Omega 3, which is found in fish, also reduces stress hormones.

It's not easy to have a healthy lifestyle all the time, especially when we have a severe mental health dis-

## Manage Stress

order, such as bipolar. I'm qualified as a personal trainer, and even I find it difficult at times. The key is consistency. People often think that a personal trainer is there to teach the top-secret exercises that will get us to meet our goals. The truth is, there's nothing a personal trainer can tell us that the internet can't. People don't need a personal trainer to know how to exercise or diet. The skill of a great personal trainer is motivating their clients to be consistent.

People often think that healthy living is about resisting temptation, which requires self-control. The truth is, people who are self-disciplined don't use self-control often. Instead, they purposely avoid situations which lead to temptation. Self-control is a limited resource. The less often we use it, the better. If we don't have sugary foods in our cupboard, we will be far less likely to eat unhealthily. When we go to the shops, if we purposely avoid aisles that are particularly tempting and go in with a shopping list, we are more likely to come out of the shop with healthy food options. After doing this, we may still have some temptation, but it would take effort to order in or go out to the shops and buy unhealthy food. We trick our brains into eating healthier by making it harder to get unhealthy food.

Likewise, people who exercise regularly don't generally rely on self-control. They have developed the habit of exercise. Habits are developed when we frequently engage in a particular behaviour for a long period of time. This makes the behaviour become automatic. When we automate behaviours, we don't need to rely on motivation anymore to get us moving.

People often give up on exercise because they think of it in black and white terms: 'I need to exercise for an hour or else there's no point'. Some days, we may not feel up to an intensive work-out. Should that one day without meeting our strict regime leave us defeated, on the verge of giving up? No. We don't need to be so hard on ourselves. Even walking to the shops rather than taking the car is healthy and beneficial. We simply need to get into the habit of regular exercise; into the habit of moving our body more than usual every day. Once we start, we may feel able to do more than we originally thought. If not, that's okay. Over time, the habit will be formed. Patience is key. People often give up on healthy living due to high expectations. By lowering them, we set ourselves up for success.

*2) Sleep well and take up relaxing activities*

Finding relaxing activities not only allows us to reduce stress, but it also helps us to sleep better. Sleep is one of the key aspects of maintaining wellness in bipolar disorder, so finding activities that can relax us is essential.

Meditation is very popular in today's age, and a lot of people feel it works wonders for them. Personally, I find meditation quite boring and I feel the need to do something rather than just sit there. For this reason, I prefer progressive muscle relaxation meditation or Tai Chi. A lot of research has shown great benefits of progressive muscle relaxation. I mentioned this form of meditation previously and I suggested to listen to some guided meditations online. They have helped me significantly, especially when I've had problems sleeping. Progressive muscle relaxation is beneficial to anyone who is experiencing stress, regardless of whether they have mental health difficulties or not, (Rausch et al., 2006).

Tai Chi is a form of martial art; however, its slow movements make it very relaxing, so it has since become an activity that people use to meditate. Tai Chi, in my experience, is perfect for mania. When we are manic, we feel the need to move, and there's nothing that I would hate more than sitting or lying down still. With Tai Chi, you can focus on your breathing and feel your body's sensations as you move. There are many tutorials online on how to conduct Tai Chi, and I would recommend them to anyone. Plenty of research has indicated the value of Tai Chi in reducing stress levels, (Sandlund et al., 2000)

I've never invested time into yoga, primarily because my flexibility is dreadful. But I know that many people feel that it has benefitted them greatly. Once we find activities that we personally find relaxing, we can begin to de-stress and prevent relapse

*3) Externalise - Seek out social support*

Keeping stress bottled up isn't healthy. One way to externalise our stress is through seeking social support, (Beehr et al., 1990). Being able to talk about our problems with a friend or a therapist can help us to relieve our stress at difficult times. Humans are social beings, and finding comfort in others is natural and helpful. Suppressing our emotions never ends well.

If we stay physically healthy, find ways to relax, and externalise our problems in healthy ways, we can feel less stressed in our day-to-day lives and protect our mental and physical health.

# CHAPTER XXI
## *Manage Anger*

If someone asked me to name the most devastating aspect of my bipolar disorder, I'd answer before they even finished their question. The volcano of anger within me left me and those I love burnt. It wasn't due to a lack of effort or self-restraint. I tried so hard to keep a lid on it. But how beneficial is a lid to a volcano? I feel an immense amount of guilt for the effect of my anger on those around me. Writing this chapter is challenging because I don't like to remember. I hurt when I think of all the times that I've burnt people I care about. I hurt when I think of all the relationships that have been ruined due to this intense volcano.

Approximately 60% of people with bipolar disorder experience sudden bouts of anger and high levels of irritability, (Perlis et al., 2004). These symptoms can occur in both mania and depression and are particularly severe in mixed states.

Anger is adaptive when experienced within the normal realm and in the right context. Its function is to show us that there is something wrong in our environment and to motivate us to do something about it. Maybe something is triggering memories of bad experiences; maybe we're in a situation that we have no control over; maybe we feel resentment towards someone that has harmed us; or maybe we're surprised and disappointed that we didn't get something we wanted. This emotion, at a healthy level, can prompt people to take action to proactively change the situation and achieve their goals.

Although anger has the potential to be adaptive, it can become damaging if experienced too intensely. In my own case, I have hurt many people with my words and behaviour. In some cases, physical confrontations can happen. When anger is too intense, our heartbeat and blood pressure rise and our muscles become tense. We feel a need to move and, in my case, a need to smash things. We also believe that this anger is justified in the situation.

I would get triggered if my Mum mentioned the religion that I was brought up in. I would get angry if a teacher forgot my name or told me off for something I didn't do. My biggest trigger for anger was if I witnessed an injustice.

An example of this was when I saw a young man in a club inappropriately touching a girl who looked scared and kept telling him to leave her alone. I put my hand on his shoulder and asked him to stop. Immediately, six young men were screaming in my face in the club. I confronted them all and shouted back. I didn't care that there were six of them; all I felt was an intense amount of anger for the abuse the girl suffered. A bouncer separated us but I was still so angry. The bouncer had to help calm me down. He said that he agreed they were wrong but that I needed to control myself or I would be kicked out. Unfortunately, I bumped into the group of young men again and we got in other confrontations. When I left the club, they were outside waiting for me. My friend Dan told me a year later that one of them was in prison and another one of them was in a critical condition after being involved in a knife fight. I was lucky I wasn't killed that night. This is just one example of how anger almost led me to lose my life.

Part of managing anger is being on the right medication, (Mammen et al., 2004). As I've said before, it's hard to keep a lid on the volcano of anger, regardless of what we do. Bipolar medication calms the mind, making it far easier to deal with anger and irritability. However, there are a number of other techniques that I've learnt which have helped me in anger management.

Retreating is a great option. If I feel intense anger, I tend to retreat to my room or a safe location and listen to music that either helps me feel understood or calms me down, depending on the severity of the anger that I feel. I don't tend to respond to people until after I have rethought the situation and cooled down.

Secondly, increasing my awareness of anger has helped me to feel anger less often. I tend to feel anger when something triggers my insecurities. Feelings of rejection and getting things wrong are triggering for me. I feel most insecure when I feel a lack of control over injustices that surround me. I want to be able to protect everyone and not being able to do that makes me feel small.

It's natural to feel anger when our insecurities are triggered. We have the biological reaction of anger when we feel that something is threatening our survival. In ancient times, people would feel insecure about their weaknesses that could risk their life or social status. They needed to fight for their survival, and their social status was important to their livelihood and that of their family. Anger helped them to become more dominant and increase their chances of survival.

In modern times, an anger response isn't generally necessary for our survival. In fact, an anger response in some situations makes it harder for us to live. Awareness of when our anger is harmful is important. Even if someone was malicious and intentionally hurt us, reacting with anger would often hurt us more than the other person. Accepting our insecurities can help us not to have to deal with this horrible emotion as often.

When I feel triggered, I tell myself that I am experiencing this anger due to my own problems with rejection, self-worth or lack of control. I accept that I have these problems because I've been rejected numerous times and have witnessed and experienced great injustices. But I accept that it's my responsibility to help myself to overcome these insecurities, rather than putting the accountability on others. In doing this, I reduce the pressures before the volcano starts erupting. However, I do believe that my medication is the primary reason why I am able to control my anger. It helps subdue the pressure and makes life a whole lot easier.

# CHAPTER XXII
## *Embrace Vulnerability*

Growing up, I was a strong believer that vulnerability was a weakness. If I wanted to be strong, I had to get rid of any insecurities within me. I would strive to become invulnerable and robotic. When I witnessed emotional outbursts around me, I viewed it as a weakness, and I vowed to never let myself show volatility. I never wanted to process my emotions; I wanted to focus on productivity and efficiency. I cared about success at any cost to myself. I viewed this as strength. I now realise how wrong I was.

I was pretty extreme in my view that vulnerability is a weakness. However, I wasn't alone in this view. Most people try to hide their insecurities. We live in a world where people post the 'best bits' of their lives on social media and edit pictures to make themselves look as good as the technology they have can allow. We live in a world where self-improvement is the new norm, and if you don't always have 'good-vibes', then you're not good company. It's as if we're all taught to put a mask on when we wake up in the morning.

## Embrace Vulnerability

Although striving for self-improvement is incredibly important and has been a massive part of my own progress, it shouldn't come at the expense of vulnerability. Brené Brown is a researcher whom I have mentioned previously. She is famous for her research on vulnerability and shame.

When first studying vulnerability, she had the preconceived view that it was a negative trait. She was brought up believing that vulnerability was a weakness and expected to find that vulnerability would have undesirable consequences. She was astounded when her results showed the opposite. She found that vulnerability not only allows us to process and move past our negative emotions, such as shame, but it also allows us to experience positive emotions and pleasure in our lives.

Trying to make ourselves invulnerable prevents us from being able to form real relationships, it prevents us from fully enjoying the activities we do, and it prevents us from loving ourselves. To love ourselves, we need to look at the man or woman in the mirror, not at a mask.

I tried for a long time to avoid being vulnerable. I couldn't help but feel vulnerable during my bipolar disorder, but I tried to hide from it. This prevented me from maximising my recovery strategies. Even after I managed to get to a point of stability, I carried on trying to be invulnerable. Perhaps if I hadn't, I wouldn't have achieved quite as much in terms of work or studies, but I felt a lack in my life. I felt a bit disconnected and down. Not so much a down mood state, but more of a feeling of not experiencing life to the full.

After watching Brené Brown's speeches on vulnerability, I took steps to feel more vulnerable and embrace my insecurities. Now, I am able to fully enjoy being with my loving girlfriend, with my loving parents and sisters, with my great friends, and most of all, with my awesome nephews. I'm incredibly grateful to George Dee, who has helped in the production of this book and who guided me to watch Brené Brown's videos. They've changed my life.

# CHAPTER XXIII
## *Replace Shame with Empathy*

Earlier in this book, I said that shame had been described as the swampland of the soul. When we feel shame, we hide away from it, and it builds and builds inside of us, affecting our relationships and everything we do. Inside, we develop this deep, dirty swamp that eats away at who we are and our ability to experience pleasure. Everything I know about shame and vulnerability I have learnt from Brené Brown, so I'll be summarising what I have learnt from her in this chapter.

True connection is powerful. I am happy and love life because I am fully present to enjoy every moment that I get to spend with those I love most. In the past, being riddled with shame prevented me from feeling these positive emotions. I would often have intrusive thoughts, picturing things I'd done wrong or things that had happened to me. As a consequence, I would be hard on myself. If someone asked me what was wrong, I'd tell them I was fine and change the topic. The ironic thing was that I experienced so much shame because of my belief that invulnerability was beneficial to my life. I was riddled with shame because of my endeavours to become 'strong'.

I wanted to be courageous, but I completely misunderstood what the word means. The original term for courage comes from the Latin word 'cor', which means heart. To be courageous meant to speak from the heart, to tell our story and be honest about it. After learning this, I had an epiphany. I always thought that to be courageous was the exact opposite – not to show anyone your insecurities. I wasn't alone in this thinking. A lot of people think that we need to mask our insecurities to be strong. However, just because something is popular opinion doesn't mean it's accurate. By having the courage to show our vulnerabilities to the world, we are able to eradicate shame and build meaningful relationships.

Brené Brown describes the ability to connect as being on a continuum. On one side is empathy and on the other is shame. She described vulnerability as the knob that determines where we fit on that continuum. If we don't embrace our vulnerability, we feel shame. If we embrace vulnerability, then we are able to feel pure empathy for others. Then, we can begin to feel a connection with others and truly care when they tell their stories. We are able to learn what the word love really means. In my opinion, there is nothing more beautiful.

In this book so far, I have mentioned a lot of things that I'm not proud of. These are things that I felt ashamed of and hid from people for many years. Now that I allow myself to feel vulnerable, I don't feel that shame anymore. In exchange for that, I feel guilt. A healthy amount of guilt for the things that I have done wrong inspires me to try and be a better man.

In making this decision, I have been given a gift. I have been given the privilege to feel empathy for everyone reading this book. I'm grateful to have learnt what it means to have empathy. I write about these insecurities and things I used to be ashamed of because I hope whoever is reading it can benefit from it. Feeling empathy allows me to enjoy my life because I don't look at people and feel jealous or resentment anymore. I look at people and feel connected. I feel like I am part of a community, and I feel a sense of belonging. It's the best gift I have ever received, so I want to thank both George Dee and Brené Brown dearly for allowing me to experience true connection.

# CHAPTER XXIV
## *Manage healthy attachments*

Attachment-based therapies have always fascinated me. The premise of attachment-based therapies is to develop or rebuild the ability to trust and have healthy relationships with others. The therapists do this by creating a model client-therapist relationship. Forming relationships is difficult for anyone. Add bipolar into the mix, or any mental disorder for that matter, and it becomes very challenging.

I struggled to have healthy attachments with people following persistent episodes of illness. Growing up, I never had problems with attachment. I am naturally quite a stoic and reserved person. Growing up, I didn't feel the need to have close relationships outside of my family. This desire grew with time, especially because, in my family, it's the norm to find your future wife or husband very early in life. For example, my parents met when my Dad was fifteen and my Mum was fourteen, and they married ten years later.

But repeated episodes of illness and my previous anger management problems have led to many

## Manage healthy attachments

breakups and fallings out. As a result, I became insecure in my attachments. Although I have improved a lot, this is still an issue today. I think the moment that affected me the most was when I was engaged to be married, and my fiancé, Katie, left me. I am scared of being left again, and it's hard to fully trust that someone won't decide to leave me. It's happened many times before, so it seems probable in my mind that it'll happen again. I do take solace, however, that the likelihood of being rejected has substantially decreased due to the stable state of mind I am now in. It was only an issue when I was going in and out of episodes, so I feel more secure when I think of it that way.

Despite being a work in progress in this department, I want to give my two cents on how I'm beginning to get better in this regard. I'm trying to make sure I take relationships and friendships at a slower pace. I don't jump into anything quickly. Instead, I let the relationship grow organically over time. I also make sure I only associate with people who seem loyal and trustworthy and give them time to prove it.

I tell myself that it is quite normal to feel scared of rejection. It's one of the most common fears experienced by humans; it's just one that most people are too ashamed to admit that they have. As social inclusion was essential to our survival in times of old, fear of rejection would increase an individual's chances to survive by motivating them to socialise and to make an effort to fit in. I used to be harsh on myself for having this fear, but now I accept it. I let myself feel vulnerable in my relationships and, in doing so, I feel a stronger sense of connection with others. It's possible to be healthy in attachments while having a slight fear that the other may leave.

I now realise that the most vital relationship I will ever have is my relationship with myself. I can finally say that I love myself for who I am. I realise I have many faults, but I accept them. I watched a TED talk recently, which helped me with my outlook on life. A very courageous lady admitted to having been divorced three times. She said that many people viewed her as a failure. She, like me, wanted nothing in life more than to get married. She wanted to create a family, and this was her primary aim.

But then, she decided to take a step back. She realised that the most important person to get married to was herself. This sounds strange at first, but it makes sense when reflected upon. Marrying myself meant deciding to love myself in sickness and in health till death do us part. It's a decision, and I believe the moment we do this, the healthier we become in our other relationships. Even if we are still scared of others leaving, it doesn't affect us quite so

*Manage healthy attachments*

much anymore. We become stable in the most important relationship of all, our relationship with ourselves. The TED talk is called 'The person you really want to marry' by Tracy McMillan.

My girlfriend, Pricilla, is a very kind and loving young woman with a loyal and trustworthy heart. She's proved this over three years of friendship. But I've decided that, regardless of what happens in this relationship, I'm going to carry on developing and working on the most important relationship in my life - my relationship with myself. Also, of primary importance is my relationship with my family and, particularly, my nephews whom I love so much.

# CHAPTER XXV
## Manage social circle

*"We are the average of the 5 people we spend the most time with."*

*Jim Rohn*

Dr David McClelland, a social psychological researcher at Harvard, said that the people we associate with most determine approximately 95% of our success and failure, (Hardy & Hardy, 2019). What we put in us determines what we create outwardly. For example, if we put healthy foods into our daily diet, then we will look healthier, feel healthier and have more energy. The same principle applies to social environments. The people around us, through their body language, their words and their actions, influence our body language, our words, and our actions.

As mentioned earlier, a sense of belonging and security in our social circle is one of the most important components for us to master for our adaptiveness. We are biologically wired to adapt and change depending on the associates that we have. As a consequence, if we surround ourselves with negative people, this will exacerbate our negativity. If we surround ourselves with drug addicts, we will be more likely to take drugs. If we surround ourselves with irresponsible people, we will become more irresponsible. In contrast, if we surround ourselves with positive people, we will become more positive. If we surround ourselves with ambitious people, we will become more ambitious. And if we surround ourselves with responsible people, we will be more responsible.

Sometimes, we might not want to be surrounded by positive people. When I'm depressed, the last thing I want is a bubbly, positive person rabbiting on about their daily activities. It can increase my irritability and leave me feeling alone, like no one understands. When depressed, I want people around who can empathise, understand and relate.

Where do we strike a balance? How do we find people who are positive and optimistic and have qualities we want to emulate, and yet are able to empathise with us? The truth is – that question is for each individual to answer. Only I can know what my balance is. Only you can know what your balance is. We all have our own values, principles and goals.

I like surrounding myself with individuals who have either experienced childhood trauma or those with mental health difficulties who are passionate about self-improvement, taking active steps towards recovery and being empathetic to those who also have mental health problems. This is the perfect balance for me - finding people who can relate through their own life experiences, but who, like me, are trying their best to develop within themselves. If we surround ourselves with people and environments which support our goals and values, we create an echo chamber, where we only listen to values, principles and life lessons which we care about on a personal level.

I attribute a lot of my successes to the mentors and individuals with mental health difficulties who have put an earnest effort into inspiring me to pursue my vision and become a psychological researcher. I'm very grateful to everyone who's in my life right now. I'm glad that I've taken steps to remove those who harm my vision and keep those in that help me progress. I hope I can help those in my social circle the same way they have helped me.

# CHAPTER XXVI
## Building our metacognitive abilities

The word metacognition means 'thinking about thinking'. It is the ability to reflect on how we think so that we respond to problems in the right way. Metacognitive awareness is vital if we want to study, hold down a job or make a career for ourselves. Bipolar often steals our ability to function. Only through building my metacognition through cognitive remediation therapy (CRT) was I able to start functioning again. According to Flavell (1979), there are three main aspects of metacognition.

*(1) Awareness of strengths and weaknesses*

It's important to develop an understanding of our strengths and weaknesses. If we know where our strengths lie, we can choose to focus on goals that align well with them. If we know what our weaknesses are, we can try to improve in those areas, ask others for advice, or we can avoid problems that exploit our weaknesses. For example, I struggle to learn foreign languages. I'm able to speak some Polish, but very little. I personally prefer to choose goals which are in line with my strengths, so I wouldn't choose to teach Polish as my career. However, if I had the goal to teach Polish, I would admit to myself that it would take me many years to become fluent. It would take a long time to get to a level where I'd be able to teach another person. If this fact didn't dissuade me from choosing this career, I would have to devote a number of years to learn this language. I would need to find an alternative way of making income in the meantime, as it would take time before meeting my goal. Of course, if our dream is to do something that we may naturally struggle with, this shouldn't dissuade us from pursuing it. But we should be realistic and take into account the amount of effort, time and resources it would take to meet that goal.

I work best alone, behind a computer screen. I'm good at understanding concepts and theories and seeing implications and limitations of them. This makes me a good fit for a career in research. There are aspects of research that I still find hard. For example, I'm not exactly the fastest of readers. Going forward in my career, I will need to take that weakness into account when I'm planning my days, allocating extra time to read papers. I also struggle with working for long periods of time. I perform the best if I work for ten-to-fifteen minutes and then take a break of equal length. I don't mind working from the moment I wake up until I sleep, as long as I can work in those intervals. Discovering this was a huge revelation for me, helping optimize my productivity. I highly recommend working out what pace and hours of the day are most suitable for your ideal efficiency.

I developed an awareness of my cognitive strengths and weaknesses by asking friends and family. I chose to ask people whom I knew were frank and honest. Most people described me as efficient, intuitive, insightful, and understanding. They said I wasn't as good at social interaction, practical tasks and memory.

The second method I used to develop an awareness of my strong points and shortcomings was by thinking back on all my biggest successes over the years. I then tried to find patterns in what it was that made me succeed in those situations. This was when I realised that my biggest successes were when I was behind a computer screen. I noticed that most of my triumphs involved science. This was also when I understood that I'm most productive when working in ten-to-fifteen minute intervals, taking breaks after a short, intensive period of work.

*Awareness of task difficulty*

As mentioned earlier, at one stage when manic, I thought it would be possible to build the biggest

Chinese organisation in the world within a matter of days. That was clearly an unrealistic idea. I grossly underestimated the difficulty and complexity of the task and how long it would take. A goal of that magnitude would require careful planning, forethought and, of course, time. If I worked for twelve hours a day consistently for forty years, made the right strategic moves and made connections within the business world, then yes, there would be a slim possibility that I would be able to achieve this. I like ambitious thinking. But there's ambition, and then there's being delusional.

Bipolar often affects our ability to understand how difficult a task is and how long it would take to accomplish. This is particularly evident when we are in the middle of an episode. However, this can often spill over and extend to periods of euthymia too. When I engaged in CRT, I would undertake certain computer tasks and would consistently miscalculate the level of difficulty and duration of the task.

I got better at understanding task difficulty by thinking back to how I'd tackled previous tasks and how long they took to complete. It took me four years of persistent practice to become good at basketball; it took five years of determined running training to become great at running, and it took me three months of four hours a day of study to ace all my exams. Remembering this helped me to develop a better awareness of how long tasks take and how difficult they are. Recording the task difficulty and length of completion of tasks as we go about our life is a great strategy for developing a realistic approach to problems.

*Awareness and application of warm thinking strategies*

When we engage in a task, we either use cold thinking strategies or warm thinking strategies. Cold thinking strategies are when we race into a task without thinking of the techniques which would be most suitable. Warm thinking strategies require more prudence and involve choosing techniques that make the task easier.

Let's say I tell you I'm going to list eight single-digit numbers and ask you to repeat them back to me in the same order. Seven, four, eight, nine, one, two, five, eight. A cold thinking strategy would be to listen carefully and then try to recall each number.

In contrast, an example of a warm thinking strategy would be to combine the single-digit numbers and reformulate them as four double-digit numbers. If you used this technique, you would say to yourself: seventy-four, eighty-nine, fifteen, and fifty-eight. This would make it easier for you to remember the eight numbers. This warm thinking strategy can be called 'chunking'.

The reason why we often use cold thinking strategies when approaching problems is that we race into them. We want to finish the task as quickly as possible and think that the best way to do so is by tackling them head-on. However, planning and taking a step back not only helps us to improve our accuracy, but it can also help us to improve our speed. I've developed this skill by allowing myself time to think of what would be the best approach to a task and plan my course of action accordingly.

-

Thanks to my CRT therapist, I was able to improve in these three areas of metacognition. This allowed me to go from not being able to read a page of a book, to be able to read and write some fiction. By developing in these areas, I was able to take the steps to finally becoming a functioning human being. Sadly, I was non-functional for a long time, and I'm grateful for finding these techniques.

Building our metacognition is not only good for our performance and functioning. It's also good for our general mental health and our self-esteem. Our self-esteem improves when we succeed, and when we know ourselves and accept ourselves. Knowing how to better approach problems also severely reduces the stress we experience as our approach makes task completion easier. I view it as the best psychological tool I have learnt regarding my functioning.

# CHAPTER XXVII
## *Getting Structure Back in My Life*

When I was a child, I loved Winnie the Pooh. I believe that children's programmes and books teach us brilliant life lessons, no matter our age. There is one episode that sticks in my mind. I may get some of the specifics wrong because this was approximately twenty years ago, but I'll try my best to recall accurately.

All the characters were in a bit of a rut. It had been raining and raining, all day, every day and, as a result, Pooh and friends were bored and seemed rather down. Rabbit, being his usual organised self, decided to show the rest of the characters how to keep a schedule. He helped them to plan out their days and think of activities that were important and could keep them busy. Over time, the characters got more structure back into their lives and started to feel happier. They accomplished a lot and felt satisfied with the work and fun activities they were doing. When the weather got better, they were happier than ever. I'm glad Rabbit's obsession with organisation finally was a benefit to the whole gang.

Building a routine to stick to in daily life helps us to get through the worst of times. How we spend each day affects how we feel. How we feel affects our mental health, our functioning and our quality of life. When I first wanted to get structure in my own life, I tried to find a routine that would help me to achieve externally. I wanted to find a schedule that allowed me to accomplish things in life, so I wouldn't feel debilitated by this illness. I wanted to be able to work and live independently. That was a good goal, but success in our careers isn't the only important goal to strive for. Now, I realise the importance of including activities which I enjoy and devoting time to spend with those I love. I feel like I've finally found a good balance. Here are the four different types of activities that I try and include in my schedule.

*(1) Activities for self-improvement*

Focussing on activities that benefit us helps us to cultivate self-love. My girlfriend feels loved when I make an effort to help her. If I comfort her when she is feeling down or massage her if she is in pain, she is able to feel some joy despite her struggles. It's because she feels valued. It's the same with ourselves. The more effort we put into bettering ourselves, the more self-love we will have and the happier we will feel. Whether we are exercising, eating vegetables, doing Tai Chi, or simply taking a shower, we are improving our self-esteem by devoting time to benefit ourselves. The most important person to show us that we are worthy is ourselves. As we develop in our self-worth, we will even notice that others treat us with more respect too.

*(2) Activities with those I love*

According to Maslow's triangle, a sense of belonging is even more of a base need than self-esteem, (Maslow & Lewis, 1987). Sometimes the last thing we want to do is socialise, especially when we're depressed. Being with others can feel draining. I know, for myself, even when I wasn't in episode, I would often feel different from others. As a consequence, I would avoid social interaction.

But it's important to have some human contact daily. Maybe it's simply playing a game together or watching a TV program. Maybe it's a family meal or a quiz night each week. Whatever it is, if we keep it up, we see benefits. My psychiatrist once wrote to my GP that I spend time watching TV with my Dad. I laughed about that, thinking 'why is this being written in a letter to my GP?' I now realise the importance of those times with my Dad. They helped me to get through some dark spells. My psychiatrist realised the importance, which is why they put it in the letter. Without that passive form of connecting to others, I would have felt far more socially isolated, and my mental health would have deteriorated further.

*(3) Activities that get us closer to meeting our goals*

A famous saying by Mary Sarton goes 'routine is not a prison, but the way to freedom from time.' If we want the freedom to enjoy success in our lives, we need to have activities that push us towards our goals. For example, to go from someone who couldn't read a book to someone who could write a book, I had to spend a lot of time reading and writing. I was fortunate that I had help through my therapist to improve in my concentration, but I needed to listen to the advice and read a lot of books to develop the skill to read faster. At the start, I was very slow, and it was difficult to concentrate, but now, I can read books and feel confident enough to write one. The goal of reading was something I put into my daily schedule, and it helped me to meet my goals.

*(4) Activities that we enjoy simply for the pleasure the activity gives*

Although it's important to strive for self-improvement and to better our relationships, we shouldn't deprive ourselves of our guilty pleasures. Showing self-love is about being kind to ourselves. Part of being kind to ourselves is sometimes engaging in activities which bring light relief and pleasure. These activities may seem pointless to others, but they are important. For example, I like listening to music, watching animated music videos on YouTube and dancing like a mad man. I find a balance where I'm able to do that for fun and still have time each day to work towards the other three goals mentioned in this chapter.

-

If we spend time enjoying the moment, strive to take part in activities which better ourselves, fill our need for belonging and bring us closer to our goals, we can live successful and happy lives. The routine I have set up for myself has given me purpose and a reason to wake up each morning. I can't remember the last day I didn't want to get out of bed.

## CHAPTER XXVIII
### *Working on my life goals*

I believe that all of us who have bipolar disorder are passionate people. Everyone whom I've met so far with this disorder has strong views and has a drive built in them that is thirsting to come out once they find stability. The more that we are able to manage our symptoms, the more we feel able to function efficiently. Once we get to this stage, I believe that we are all highly capable of striving for our dreams and accomplishing really awesome things.

Passion is a term that is used frequently in modern times. 'Quit your nine-to-five and follow your dreams' is the new trendy thing to do. For a lot of people, it works, and they find great pleasure in developing that independence. However, I believe that modern culture has altered our concept of what passion actually is.

Passion can be anything. It could be owning a sports brand, spending time with family, saving money to travel the world or fervently following our religious beliefs. Following our passion doesn't necessarily mean we need to quit our job and become self-employed. My best friend told me that he admires that I have chosen a career path that I feel passionately about. But I turned around to him and said that he's found his passion too. He enjoys powerlifting. He goes to a professional strongman gym and has met great friends there. He is always striving to improve himself in the gym and finds great pleasure in the process. Finding the goals that we want to focus on in our life is down to us. There is no set way of going about finding our passion. But I want to describe how it was when I found mine and how it gives me great contentment.

When I was at my lowest point, I viewed suicide as the best possible outcome for both myself and everyone around me. Slowly, I took steps to develop my ability to function and engage in activities that were good for me. One of them was YouTubing. I became a YouTuber talking about mental health topics and greatly enjoyed meeting other YouTubers and watchers, two of whom I'm still in contact with today. One of these was my ex-fiancé, Katie. We grew close quickly. We shared a lot of the same psychological problems and could understand each other. But her experiences and her mental health were far more extreme than my own. Yet I saw a beauty and a love in her that I had never seen in anyone before. I looked at her, and I thought to myself – I want to spend my life finding and trying to help people like her. I had never felt a sense of belonging before. I finally felt I had found my people, my sense of belonging.

This is why I decided to work in the mental health field and to become a psychological researcher. I want to help people like Katie, who are so beautiful inside and yet are too ill to get what they deserve – a life they can enjoy. I want to help other people, whom I believe are far more deserving than me, to enjoy life to the full. That is my passion.

Does that mean that I always enjoy sitting down reading psychology books? Does it mean that I always get on with colleagues in the mental health industry who clearly don't care as much as they should? Does it always mean that I find my work easy? Definitely not. But for me, finding my passion means fighting for something that I believe in, and the sense of purpose has fuelled me in my life.

Overcoming bipolar disorder isn't just about reducing symptoms. It's about learning to love life. Mental illness strips that from us. It strips both our self-love and our love of life. By finding our passion and working towards it, we can regain our zest for life. I believe the things we care about most drive our passion. I think realising that it doesn't have to be a career path opens up lots of possibilities and will help people live happier lives.

# CHAPTER XXIX
## *Slow and steady wins the race*

Growing up, I never liked the story of the Tortoise and the Hare. I think this is partly because I didn't agree with the premise. I thought to myself, why don't we just go at a balanced pace? Why do we need the extremes of the hare or the tortoise? Why don't we run at a comfortable rate that we can maintain? I still believe that this is the case in many respects. However, I now see the importance of emulating the tortoise in some scenarios.

Sometimes it's impossible to run without negative consequences. Some situations are so arduous that it's as if we're in deep, muddy water. If we try to run or even walk at a fast pace, we are likely to fall over and it would take us a long time to get back up again. If we take it very slowly and move carefully through the treacherous terrain, we can make progress.

This is certainly the case in a disorder as severe as bipolar. Sometimes I'd make the decision to rapidly beat my illness. I'd form a good regimen with food, exercise and relaxation techniques. I'd get in a flow

## Working on my life goals

of working towards self-improvement, going at a fast rate, trying my best to beat this as fast as I could. After a few months of stability, I'd question whether I needed medication anymore. I really thought I'd beaten bipolar. My efforts deserved commendation as I tried really hard. However, I was foolish to think that I could overcome bipolar so quickly. I would always fall flat on my face and would feel so frustrated with myself for 'failing'. I later realised that the tortoise approach was needed, and it has worked very well for me.

This section, although short, has a lot of information packed into it. I'm fortunate to have many great mentors around me to teach me these concepts and an amazing family who have been supportive, allowing me to devote a lot of energy to my recovery. However, it hasn't been a quick journey. I've accumulated this information over the past ten years. Those ten years felt like sixty. But I'm glad I started following the tortoise philosophy after a few years of racing like a hare. If I hadn't, it would have probably taken far longer than ten years to start winning the war.

For all those with bipolar disorder, I believe in you. You can break free. I hope my own journey of trying to become my own psychologist can inspire you in yours. Within this section, we've looked into CBT tactics that can be used to spot triggers, early warning signs of episodes and how to create action plans that can help us prevent episodes. We've recognised the importance of journaling for self-awareness, expression, and self-development. We've identified stress management techniques, how to improve ourselves and our relationships, and the power of accepting our vulnerabilities. Finally, we discovered how to improve our metacognition and how to proactively develop, grow, and succeed in our goals whilst enjoying the process.

In this slow journey towards recovery, we need to be consistent. This is difficult. I have failed many times in keeping my efforts consistent, but I'm glad that I've finally got to a stage where I am able to work steadily towards my own recovery and maintenance of my illness. In the next section, we will be taking a look at consistency, what it means in bipolar disorder and the steps that I took to become consistent in my own journey.

# Section 4:
# Consistency, Consistency and more Consistency

# CHAPTER XXX
*Why is consistency so important?*

Bipolar is a disorder of extremes. We go through the extreme highs of mania, where we are oozing enthusiasm, irritability and grandiosity. Then we go through extreme lows of depression, where pleasure is a term we no longer understand; we feel lethargic and defeated. This bipolarity can lead to great problems with our self-awareness and make it hard to manage our illness, our relationships and our life goals.

How do we manage our illness if we forget who we are and what episodes of illness look like? How do we manage our illness if we are inconsistent in taking our medication? How do we stay consistent in our behaviour if the social influences we have surrounding us are always changing? And how do we progress in life if we are constantly changing our life goals?

All of these questions are hurdles which I've tripped over many times. I've repeatedly forgotten who I am and what bipolar is, been inconsistent with medication, had on-off relationships and have

*Why is consistency so important?*

changed my path in life many times over. It took a rather long time to find consistency. In this section, I'll be revealing how I managed to improve in this way.

Bipolar is a mood disorder that is, by nature, inconsistent. As a result, it can create many inner conflicts within the self, regardless of an individual's disposition prior to getting into episodes. Growing up, people always described me as stoic and almost robotic. I was consistent. I never had many variations in my viewpoints, my life goals, or my self-awareness. Bipolar turned that all around and I became an inconsistent person.

I hope this section can help you to develop a deeper understanding of consistency, show you the importance of it and some strategies that I have used to become more consistent in my life. We will start by discussing the importance of being consistent with medication.

# CHAPTER XXXI
## *Consistency in medication*

When I first discussed medication in this book, I mentioned a couple of quotes from Kanye West. I love Kanye; he's one of my favourite musicians, and I view him as a creative genius. Despite his bipolar disorder, he has been very successful in his career and has been a great influence on other artists, as well as his fans. I am deeply saddened that during the writing of this book, he was turned into an internet meme and viewed as a crazy joke. He announced on American Independence Day 2020 that he would be running for President. His campaign has been 'different', to say the least. He even cried and screamed during his own presidential rally.

Kanye's manic episodes are extreme. I feel like I can relate to his bipolar illness in a lot of ways. If I was in the public eye when I was most ill, I think my behaviour would have been even more erratic, as the stress of being in the limelight and the constant critique would unquestionably add extra strain to an already difficult mental illness. Although I don't always believe the stories published in tabloid

## Consistency in medication

magazines, reports claim that his wife and friends say that he's been refusing to take his medication. It wouldn't be surprising at all, judging by his behaviour. Refusing to take bipolar medication or missing doses can have devastating effects on the sufferer and their loved ones. I have myself experienced this first-hand, and I'm sorry for the effect this decision had on my friends and family.

I'd be lying if I said that I've never skipped a dose of medication. It seems to be a universal rule. Almost all of us have done it at some stage or another. I can't count the number of times that my family, friends, and doctors have face palmed in total exasperation at boastful statements I made like "I've fixed myself" or "I don't have bipolar disorder". It's easy to see that this line of thinking could, at times, lead me to the decision to come off my medication. Why would I need medication when there is nothing wrong with me? Obviously, this never ended well. Every time it happened, I'd regret it within a few weeks. I'd go into a mixed episode, have fits of anger, become suicidal, and end up in the hospital. Somehow, I'd never learned my lesson. I think it happened three times.

Sometimes, even when we realise the importance of medication and are dedicated to our care, we may forget to take it. Taking medication daily seems to become an automatism; it's something that is incorporated into our daily routine, like making the bed or brushing our teeth. We can get so caught up in our busy lives that sometimes these day-to-day activities seem to slip through the cracks. Every now and then, I'd stare at my med box, trying to work out whether I'd taken my dose yet. I would go through and count how many pills were left and try to figure out whether I'd missed a dose. Usually, my Mum would remember the amount of medication there should have been. She's always had an elephant's memory, unlike me. But we're only human, and occasionally we get it wrong. I've probably forgotten to take my medications once every few months, and there have been a few instances where I've accidentally double-dosed. There's a good reason why all medication information leaflets warn against double-dosing – it can be very dangerous and is never a good idea. The advice given by doctors is often to miss the dose if uncertain whether one has taken it, and I follow this principle now.

Some people keep their medication in pill boxes so that they take the right dose. I also create my own MAR Sheet. A MAR Sheet is often used in care homes. We tick off a box whenever the time comes for us to take our medication each day, and in doing so, we make sure we make no errors in dosage.

## Consistency in medication

Being consistent with our medication can also enhance our cognitive functioning. Many people are concerned when they take medication; they may experience lethargy that often leads to fogginess and problems with creativity. However, with the regular taking of the medication, these types of side effects begin to dissipate. In their place, the rewards begin to shine through. For example, studies have shown that cognitive performance improves in patients with psychosis who take quetiapine for an extended period of time, (Akdede et al., 2005). This means that medication can have a significant positive effect on our concentration, memory, and problem-solving skills long term.

This has certainly been the case for me. I function better than ever. Quetiapine has helped me to alleviate the cognitive deficits that often happen as a consequence of prolonged and untreated bipolar disorder and has helped me to live life optimally. However, each and every one of us has a unique brain; what works for one person may be unsuitable for someone else. You and your doctor must collaborate in finding the right medications for you. We're all unique, and we each have our own journey with this disorder. Personally, quetiapine helps me not to go into mania, to balance my mood and improve my cognition, while lamotrigine helps to prevent me from entering a depression. Each person's medication combo will be different, but with consistent effort, we can find the ones that will work for us.

How do we stay consistent with our medication when we are still in the trial and error state; still trying to find the ones that work for us? Sometimes, the side effects are too much to handle. For example, when I was on a very large dose of sodium valproate, my energy level was completely depleted, and I fell into depression. Another medication led me to have severe levels of irritability and restlessness prior to going to bed. I became fearful that I wouldn't fall asleep the moment I took it, and my brain felt like it was on fire.

Unless the side effects are severe and intolerable, or even dangerous, remaining consistent on each medication for a few months has worked well for me. If the side effects don't go away but get worse or become unbearable, it is imperative that we communicate this to our physicians. They can then help us to try another option or make an adjustment to our current dose. If we notice a long period of euthymia following taking a particular medication, in my experience, the medication is good for us. Minor side effects, such as some lethargy, tend to pass with patience and time. By staying steady on each medication I tried, I was able to gauge how much the medication was benefitting me or not. I wouldn't have been able to know this if I was capricious with the

## Consistency in medication

medication prescribed to me. Staying consistent in our search for the right medications is difficult, but worth it. We need to have faith that we will find one that works for us and see the value in that.

Consistency with medication is one of the most important parts of overcoming bipolar disorder and managing the illness to a level where we can enjoy life. There are, of course, other aspects of relapse prevention that are also of vital importance.

# CHAPTER XXXII
## *Consistency in relapse prevention*

Knowing our triggers and our early symptoms helps us to create action plans. This allows us to proactively take steps to prevent relapse. This knowledge is powerful and vital in our recovery journey. However, knowledge alone isn't enough. We need to take action. That's why it's called an action plan. We need to consistently stay alert to potential triggers and symptoms and respond accordingly. This isn't always easy.

Sometimes I've been strict with myself, making sure I do everything possible to aid recovery. At other times, I couldn't care less. This is becoming a recurring topic of discussion within this book because it is a recurring theme in my own and other's experience of bipolar. Sometimes, we completely forget how severe our illness is and abandon all the recovery work we have done, assuming that we're okay now. This is one of the primary causes of relapse. Since receiving treatment, I'd say that three of the seven manic episodes I've had wouldn't have happened if I had realised the truth. The truth that beating bipolar isn't easy, and I need to consistently stay on guard.

It takes a lot of motivation and effort to want to stay consistent in relapse prevention. Nothing good in life comes easy. To have the motivation to overcome any challenge, we need to focus on why we want to win. We need to know the repercussions of not winning and the rewards we will reap from our efforts. Here are a couple of strategies that have helped me to stay motivated and consistent.

*Notice boards – priming recovery*

I have a noticeboard which I pass every time I go in and out of my room. I used to put my calendar and some pictures on it, but one day, I decided to put two poems up there. I wrote one of them when I was manic and the other when I was depressed. I liked the poems a lot, and I was proud of them. I felt like they strongly portrayed my pain and suffering. Every time I walked in and out of my room, I would see these poems. They helped me to remember the massive, rocky mountain I had overcome. It reminded me that I don't want to have to climb up it again; that I'll do anything to ensure that I'm never put in that situation again.

I quickly realised how useful it was to have the poems on the noticeboard. I asked myself, can I use the same technique for my action plans? I decided to try it out. I put a couple of sheets of paper on my noticeboard, outlining my triggers, early symptoms, and what I should do if I see things going downhill. Seeing my action plans each morning when I woke and each night as I went to bed, primed me to always take note of my mental health and to stay consistent in my recovery.

A lot of top students use this technique in their exams when they want to remember vital information that they tend to forget. They put up some notes or even just a word on their walls to make sure they remember things that they are struggling to put into their long-term memory. It's a strategy that works very well as we associate that important concept with a familiar location, for example, our bedroom. This creates more connections in our brain, helping us to recall that information easily. Using a similar principle for self-awareness has helped me to be consistent in relapse prevention.

*What are we fighting for?*

Trudging for years through the thick mud of bipolar disorder is difficult. Perhaps it's not surprising that we often feel like giving up. What's the point of always pushing our body to the limit, trudging through the mud, when each day, each week, each month, each year, we look down, and we're still deep in the mud?

## Consistency in relapse prevention

I guess, to escape that situation, we need to envision what it is we are fighting for. For me, at the start, I fought each day because I didn't want to let my family down. I wanted to be the son my parents deserved and the brother that my sisters deserved. This inspired me. Not wanting to hurt my family was a strong motivator.

Now, after a number of years of stability, my motivation is more positive. The happy event of the birth of my nephew, Max, unfortunately coincided with one of the most difficult stages in my mental health journey. I was suicidal. It was the most suicidal I've ever been. Now, he's a big boy. I love him very much. He's a lovely person, and I'm very proud of him. One day, a play date taunted Max, saying: "Only the cool kids can play here". Max replied: "I am cool actually because I have my Uncle Sam and he's really cool". This touched my heart deeply. I look at Max and see someone I want to have a positive impact on.

I carry on my fight against bipolar for my cause, wanting to support and help people who have mental health issues. I also want to keep on succeeding so that I can make my family proud of me for carrying on with my life despite going through a very difficult decade. I do it to prove to all my haters who said I wouldn't amount to anything, that I will make a success of my life.

Whatever our motivation is, as long as it's strong enough to make trudging through the mud worth it, it's a good motivation in my view. To be a fighter, we need a reason to fight. In the UFC, Joe Rogan once said: "Great fighters need great fighters". Bipolar has got a hard punch that can knock anyone down. We need to put our guard up and use the right strategies to bring it down to its knees.

# CHAPTER XXXIII
## *Consistency in our relationships*

As mentioned earlier, my relationships have been strained in recent years. It's pained me deeply, and it's been one of the most difficult consequences of my bipolar disorder. Depressive slumps have often ended in my heart being broken. The girls I've dated tend to get bored and frustrated with my lack of interest in anything. They put up with it for a while, but because my depressive episodes last for approximately six months, they tend to give up. They fell in love, for the most part, with my manic self. They loved my energy, my passion and my zest for life.

Often, friends I met in periods of stability or periods of mania lacked empathy and had no sympathy for people with insecurities. Because I viewed vulnerability as a weakness in the past, I attracted people like that; people who had very little respect for those with mental health difficulties. Not surprisingly, once I was depressed, they viewed me as weak as my insecurities were visible for everyone to see. They no longer viewed me as strong and courageous, and abandoned me.

I've had friends that I've met during depressive episodes. These friends tended to suffer from depression themselves, and we related to each other's dark thoughts. However, when I became stable, these friends often felt alone in my company because there wasn't that same connection between us anymore. We drifted apart.

Now that I've found stability, I don't have these ups and downs in my relationships. Winning the war against bipolar has given me the gift of true connection. I now only associate with people who appreciate me for the person I am and admire me for persevering in my struggle, not in spite of it. My friends are consistent in their view and treatment towards me. My stability also allows me to be a consistent friend.

However, the numerous relationship breakdowns I've had over the years have left me scarred. I've had many people I care deeply about leave me during the course of my illness, and I miss them greatly. I only feel attracted to women with a good heart, but often, my mental state was simply too much for them. Fortunately, now I'm able to have great relationships with people who accept me for who I am.

These are the six steps I've used to develop consistency in my relationship: (1) being myself from the get-go (2) sharing my vulnerabilities (3) showing empathy (4) always striving towards recovery (5) finding friends who fully respect me and (6) showing respect to others. I will now discuss each of these in turn.

## (1) Be myself from the get-go

We live in a world where we're taught to hide behind a mask. We're taught to value putting out 'good vibes' over being honest. We live in a world where narcissistic traits are respected and aspired to. We're taught to people-please and follow the crowd. It's the culture of today's age, and it's turning people into chameleons.

Being who we are is powerful. As humans, we are all unique and beautiful. If we were all the same, this world would be a boring place. Realising that and embracing who I am has added colour to my surroundings and has increased the respect that I receive from others.

Having mental health difficulties makes being ourselves particularly hard. We may want to hide away from our struggles. We may feel ashamed of our battle scars. However, putting on a mask can make our mental health worse. If we have a mask on for too long, we can forget the person behind it. As mentioned previously, knowing who we truly are is vital to our recovery and satisfaction. Knowing this and doing it are totally different things. We've all heard that we need to embrace who we are. We've all heard that we need to be ourselves. There was one thing I needed to fully accept for me to start being myself and not caring what others think.

The harsh truth we need to learn is that not everyone will like us. We can't please everyone. A lot of people won't like us for who we are. Certain people won't respect our battle scars. But who cares what those people think? Being myself has allowed the right people to come into my life. The right people are those who love me for who I am and respect me for my journey. There are many who don't like me. I focus on the people who do.

*(2) Sharing my vulnerabilities*

As Brené Brown said, vulnerability is the knob which decides where we fall on the connectedness scale; where we fall between shame and empathy. Wearing my insecurities on my sleeve gives me the power to truly connect. When I didn't do this, my relationships felt fake. They may have been stable, but I didn't enjoy the friendships as much as I could have. Now that I finally accept my vulnerabilities, I can finally enjoy the company of others. I strongly recommend, whether you have bipolar or not, to watch the videos of Brené Brown and let them help you to accept yourself and embrace your vulnerability. The impact on relationships and contentment is unsurpassable.

*(3) Showing empathy*

When we show empathy to others, we feel more connected to them, and they feel more comfortable with us. People love to feel heard. So, if we listen to others, not only will we feel more empathetic to their situations, they will also show us more love. Embracing my vulnerabilities has helped me substantially with this. But it's not always natural. I also make an effort to show empathy. I try to put myself in the other person's shoes. It's a decision, but one that creates long-lasting, healthy relationships.

*(4) Always striving towards recovery and positivity*

We all want to be surrounded by people who make us feel good. It's part of being human. This principle has inspired the 'good-vibes' movement; the positivity we put in the world causes positivity to come back to us. However, it's unrealistic to think we can be positive all the time. It would require a thick mask to be plastered onto our face. It wouldn't be real positivity, and it wouldn't be healthy.

Sometimes, I feel negative, and that's okay. I've learnt that strength comes from showing our vulnerabilities, but striving to improve; allowing ourselves to feel insecure, yet making efforts to boost our self-esteem; embracing how we feel, but making an effort to improve our overall mood and response to situations. People respect us if they see that we struggle and yet never stop trying. When we work towards our goals despite setbacks, we inspire those around us. I'm happy that my journey and philosophy of life inspires my wonderful girlfriend, Pricilla, my family and friends. Pricilla, in particular, is very supportive of my goals, and it's great to have a partner who shares my vision.

## (5) Finding friends who truly respect me

Although following the previous four points will significantly increase the likelihood of people respecting us, some people simply won't. To respect someone isn't just a feeling, it's shown in action. If a friend repeatedly treats us badly without showing us that they are truly apologetic, they don't deserve to be in our lives. We show self-respect by only associating with people who respect us. A person who respects us may make mistakes at times but, for the most part, they will try to build us up, make us feel good about our achievements and show us love, especially during periods of hardship. Removing all the people from my life who disrespected me and intentionally put me down, has helped me substantially in my own recovery and happiness.

## (6) Respecting others

A turning point in my life was when I realised that I would never be respected unless I respected others. We get back what we put in, and we need to take accountability for our own behaviour. I was never deliberately disrespectful to people, but I was so absorbed in my own illness that I often forgot that other people have feelings too.

The more we allow ourselves to feel vulnerable, the less judgmental and the more empathetic we will be of others. Brené Brown says the less vulnerability we allow ourselves to feel, the more the shame of others triggers our own shame. This leads to disconnection. Working through our shame and accepting our vulnerabilities can help us to respect others.

My relationships are the most pleasurable aspect of my life now. This certainly wasn't the case in the past. I'm grateful for the work of Brené Brown for showing me the way to embrace vulnerability as I now see all the beautiful colours that relationships have to offer.

# CHAPTER XXXIV
## *Consistency despite hardships*

Last summer, I had the biggest test of my recovery journey to date. For a year, I had been working full time whilst studying full time. This decision wasn't due to a manic episode; it was because I was trying to save money for my wedding. Although it was a challenge, I enjoyed the job. I was working in the mental health field and spent a lot of time with clients with a range of mental health difficulties.

I was offered a position with more responsibility. I was to be a deputy manager across two different services, and my main role was to work with clients who were suicidal. I was excited about this position as I felt I could make a difference. I wanted to start working in this position after my final exams; however, they were short of staff, so I had to start slightly earlier than I would have wished.

Three weeks into the job, as I was just starting to get warmed up and exams were about to begin, two massive tests came my way. Firstly, my sister Zosia became very ill. She was pregnant and almost lost her own life as well as the life of her baby. The very

## Consistency despite hardships

same week, my ex-fiancé, Katie, decided to leave me. This was a week before my final exams.

Naturally, this affected my work. I was still great with the clients; I prioritised working with them over anything. However, I became far more disorganised, was very poor at timekeeping and wasn't filling out paperwork properly. I told my manager about everything that was happening in my life, and she acted as if she cared. She said that she understood and that I could take time off if I needed to.

I took my exams. It was unbelievably difficult and stressful because I wanted to maintain my top grades, and I was finding it difficult to concentrate. There were too many things to think about. I took a few days off as sick leave and after doing so, received a thick envelope in the post. I opened it, unsure of what it would be. It consisted of approximately fifty pages of 'evidence' against me, listing all the ways that I'd failed in keeping up with my responsibilities at work: how I was poor at timekeeping, not a good team player, not filling out paperwork correctly etc. My manager even used a supervision I had with her in private against me, as I had opened up to her because I thought she genuinely cared. This hurt me deeply as there is nothing that I enjoy more than working in the mental health field. The situation was overwhelmingly triggering for me. This is a workplace in the mental health field; it was incredulous that they were so inconsiderate of a staff member who was going through a hard time themselves.

Naturally, I was concerned about relapsing. This situation was the most difficult situation I had been in since my other sister, Laura, had leukaemia. My sister almost dying, my fiancé leaving me, and work treating me with no respect was a lot to deal with. On top of this, I was already in a difficult situation with exams and with my new demanding job. I went to see my psychiatrist because I wanted to make sure I didn't go into a full-blown episode. He upped my medication for the short term as I was insistent that I wanted to do everything in my power to prevent myself having a relapse.

I decided to leave the work position, but I managed to do great in my exams despite the circumstances. I also managed to stop myself from going into an episode, even though I saw early symptoms that could lead to a mixed episode coming my way. My action plan worked, and I'm really glad that it did. However, this didn't mean this situation didn't affect me. Anyone would be affected.

My self-esteem plummeted. I felt like I had failed in my job. I felt like I failed in my relationship. I don't like failing in anything, and this made me feel as if I'd failed myself in every area of my life. I went back to my psychiatrist for a follow-up appointment, and when I told him I thought this way, he told me that I dealt with this situation far better than most healthy people would have done. This made me feel much better about myself and made me feel proud of my journey. It's one thing to cope well and stay healthy when things are going well. It's an entirely different one when things are going dreadfully.

My relationship breakup wasn't due to my own mental health problems for once. It was my partner's problems which caused her to end the relationship. I'm glad I can find solace in that fact. Also, I can find solace in the fact that I really tried as hard as I could to do well in my job. My performance was affected, but it would have been for anyone. The clients felt my support and help when I was there and showed their gratitude towards me. I'm pleased I managed to benefit them.

I'm glad that I came out of the situation well. However, there are a number of things that I would have done differently to stop that period of time from being as difficult as it was. There were also things that I learnt about myself from the situation.

Firstly, I realised that managing bipolar disorder isn't about maintaining a neutral mood at all times. Sometimes, bad times will come. Maybe it's the death of a loved one or the end of a relationship. If these types of situations don't affect us, then there is something wrong with us. We'd have to be a psychopath or wear a mask so tight that we don't feel anymore.

In the past, I perceived recovery as always keeping myself level. We all have fluctuations in mood; it's part of the beauty of the human condition. Bipolar mood swings are outside of the normal realm; however, mood fluctuations are healthy. We shouldn't be hard on ourselves for feeling low or for feeling high. We should take precautions to make sure we don't go too high or too low, but we should also accept that we are human. We all respond to situations around us. Without the normal fluctuations of life, we wouldn't be experiencing life fully.

Secondly, I learnt that I shouldn't be putting myself in situations where I am just about managing. Working whilst studying is difficult for anyone and especially in the type of work I was doing in the mental health field. I was doing it to save money for the life I was going to have with Katie, but I should have been more patient and taken it slower. I was able to work and study without any consequences before all the problems in my personal life began, but I wish I hadn't put too much pressure on myself. If I had left more room in my life for other circumstances which could come and interfere, perhaps there wouldn't have been as much of a scare of relapse.

Thirdly, and most importantly, I realised that I had grown to manage my illness. It was my first massive test of my mental resilience since my recovery journey, and I'm very proud of myself for carrying on despite hardships. It's very reassuring and gives me more confidence that I can avoid relapse in the future following other difficult circumstances that may come my way.

# CHAPTER XXXV
## *Consistency in my life goals*

Earlier this year, I decided to make a poster. I wanted to make something that inspired me. Something that I could have in my room to remind me of the positive direction that I want to walk in for the rest of my life. I envisioned a poster to be showing stars in the sky, symbolising that now that I've overcome this mountain, the stars are my limit. I wanted to use a quote that I found motivating and thought it would be more meaningful if the words came from my heart. I decided to write a short sentence to encapsulate my feelings towards my life goals. I pondered a while on it, thinking of how I could best get my feelings across. In the end, this is what I came up with:

*'When you fight for something important enough, no matter how hard times get, you will always be content.'*

I hold this philosophy of life close to my heart. No matter how hard times get, I am always content because I fight for something that I believe in. Seeing that every day when I wake and every time I go to sleep reminds me that, no matter how bored or up-

*Consistency in my life goals*

set or frustrated I may be, I'm living a life that I love and a life that is meaningful to me.

I was brought up religious. I don't believe in God anymore, but deeply respect everyone who does and follows what they believe. What I learnt from my upbringing was that believing in something bigger than myself gives me great pleasure and contentment.

I believe in all of those with bipolar disorder who are fighting every day. I believe in everyone who suffers in life or has experienced traumatic childhoods. I believe in the loved ones of those with mental health issues as they are on a difficult journey too. I believe in psychologists and psychiatrists, who dedicate their lives to helping others. I believe in all humans as we all have our own journey in life with its own challenges.

These beliefs may seem altruistic in ways, but the truth is, they are beneficial to me. Believing in something much bigger than myself and wanting to help those that suffer helps me. It gives my life more meaning and provides a really strong motivation that leaves me excited about life every single day, even when I'm suffering.

As mentioned in Section 1, I've had many massive life goals over the course of my bipolar disorder, most of which have never come to fruition. I've never become the most successful man in China; I've not become a famous rapper in Detroit; I haven't run around the world with a tent on my back and appeared on international news. Although I laugh about these goals now, I really believed at the time that these goals would be attainable. A sad thing in bipolar disorder is that, especially in mania, we have goals which we abandon when we realise they are unrealistic or that it was only something we cared about for a short period of time.

Sometimes, this tendency can continue through periods of euthymia. Due to issues in metacognition, we sometimes make leaps in our judgements and decisions on things without fully thinking them through. This can lead to persistent problems in choosing life goals.

In our recovery journey, we don't only want to avoid episodes. We want to be alive. We want to be able to say that we enjoy our life. In Section 3, I mentioned what I believe it means to find our passion. Whatever we care about or enjoy, staying consistent in it can help us live a full and beautiful life. We want to see all the colours life has to offer. We want to succeed in things we care about and see things through. My Dad always used to tell me, without effort, there's no achievement, and with no achievement, there is no satisfaction. Everything in life takes effort. Relationships, careers, and hobbies are all things that take our time and resources. By putting our energy and effort in things we care about, we achieve what we desire and are able to experience satisfaction. Nothing in life comes easy.

Once we have achieved a level of stability and maintained it for a couple of years; once we've worked on our metacognition to a degree where we think things through before we make big decisions; once we fully accept ourselves and our vulnerabilities, we can begin to make good choices regarding our life goals. Perhaps it's having a family, writing a book, making enough money to be able to travel, entering a career that we care about, or maybe it's starting a business in an industry we are passionate about.

I'm a firm believer that my life goals have helped me to get to a point where I don't just manage, but I love life. Life isn't always easy. Sometimes I hate studying. Sometimes I hate working in the mental health industry with workers who don't care or understand mental health in the way they should. But no matter how difficult it is, there's inner contentment knowing that I am doing something that I care about.

Soul searching and finding out who I am is what taught me my life goals. It came from within. For me, I want a family, and I want to be an academic, working in the mental health system. The way I was brought up, the personality I have, and my life experiences and views have led me to a position where those are the things I care most about.

It took a long time for me to find this. The people around me and a period of reflection and meditation helped me find my life goals. Without them, I wouldn't enjoy life nearly as much as I do now.

Once we find a cause or passion, how do we stick with it? Once we've become consistent in everything else previously described within this section, I believe it comes down to one thing: daily decisions. Every day, we must decide upon small goals, which, to many, may seem insignificant. However, by consistently taking small steps towards our bigger goals, we can achieve truly great things.

We can illustrate this with the big goal of building a house. That goal is achieved by laying one brick at a time in its correct position. The goal of placing a brick correctly is important, but the task is not as daunting as completing the entire house. Each brick placed is a step towards achieving our main goal. This example came from Will Smith in an interview. That interview was so inspiring to me that this image has stayed in my mind to this day.

Motivation comes and goes. No matter how hard we try, we can't feel motivated all the time. Fortu-

## Consistency in my life goals

nately, the secret to success is: we don't need motivation; all we need is to get into good habits. By forcing ourselves to lay one brick firmly on the ground each day, the task soon becomes habitual. Laying a brick on the ground becomes automatic, requiring virtually no motivation.

Every day, I set myself goals. Small goals that get me one step closer to achieving my biggest goals. I write these in my schedule. For example, today, I recorded the goal to write at least five hundred words for this book. Some days, I don't feel able to do anything because I feel sad or have something else on my mind. But I make sure I always have time to lay at least one brick. When I hit one of these small goals, I tick it off with a smiley face. Then I may reward my behaviour with chocolate or by watching something I really like.

What happens if we feel we can't concentrate? Five years ago, concentration was a big problem in my life. To some extent, it still is. I work best in five-to-fifteen minute increments, followed by a break of similar length. I then repeat. Slowly, like a tortoise, I waddle towards my goals.

There is one TED talk that stands out to me as enlightening for anyone struggling with concentration. The talk was by Stephen Duneier, and it's called How to Achieve Your Most Ambitious Goals.

I strongly recommend watching this as it's very inspiring – showing that small steps are the way to become successful in anything. We don't need to be the most talented. We just need to make little steps in the right direction. He says if you struggle to read a page of a book, start by reading one word. You'll likely feel able to read a second word. Maybe you can read a sentence. Then, if you slowly read one sentence at a time, taking a few seconds break at a time, you manage to read the full page.

By setting goals, meeting them and rewarding them, we are creating a habit of productivity and consistency. After years of effort, setting daily goals and meeting them has become automatic for me. I don't need motivation anymore to do what I need to do. Habits are powerful. The more good habits we create by planning, enacting and rewarding regularly, the more productive we will become.

In this Section, we've looked at consistency in relapse prevention, showing that consistency in both medication and psychological strategies has been important for the maintenance of my recovery We then looked at consistency in relationships and life goals, two areas that can transform our lives from being about managing our illness to having fulfilling and enjoyable lives. I hope you have learnt something here from my experience that can help you in your own journey, regardless of whether you have bipolar, are a loved one, or a mental health professional. A lot of these principles can be applied to anyone and the struggles they face.

# CHAPTER XXXVI
*A Note to those with bipolar disorder: Please remember that you are worthy and that you are awesome*

At the beginning of this book, I told the story of what a research psychiatrist, Sameer, told me when I was first diagnosed with bipolar disorder. We were sitting together in a taxi as I was a research participant in his trial, and he told me something that has stuck with me until today. I'm sure it will stay with me forever. He told me that he believed in me, and I would make a full recovery. He told me that what I was suffering was horrendous and painful and that I, like most people with bipolar disorder, am able to have many successes in life. More importantly, he said that I would be able to live a happy life, once I find the right medication and the right strategies.

He gave me the example of Kay Jamison, a leader in bipolar research and a writer of many books. He told me of her journey with bipolar disorder; that she managed to reach a level of stability within her own life and enjoy the fruits of her labour.

*Please remember that you are worthy and that you are awesome*

At times, I didn't believe Sameer. I was certain that I would always remain in a disabled state, unable to function and destined to have a life oscillating between episodes of highs and lows. When I was unable to read a page of a book, I thought it would be impossible for me to ever finish reading an entire book. Now, I have written one.

A lot of you probably haven't been as lucky as I am. I've been fortunate to have someone tell me that I am capable and worthy. I wanted to do that for you. You are awesome. You are worthy. You have been dealt a very difficult hand with bipolar disorder, but you are more than able to jump that hurdle, and once you do, you will live a life of joy and success. I believe in you and will always be rooting for you.

# CHAPTER XXXVII
## *My Dad's Speech:*
## *To all the loved ones and mental health professionals out there*

I wanted to finish this book by personally thanking my loved ones and the mental health professionals who have helped me. Thanks to this group of people, I have managed to find a life of love and pleasure. I mentioned in the forward of this book, a speech that my Dad made when I graduated from University. He was tipsy, and it was slightly embarrassing, but I enjoyed it at the same time. Here is the speech that he made:

*"Now, when you finished school and your A-Levels. When we think of where you were then, and how you were, and then the next few years. To think you are at this stage now, we wouldn't have dreamed of it. I don't think you would have dreamed of it. It was impossible from where you were. And so, for you to get to this stage, there are a couple of people that I'd like to thank. One of them is here one of them isn't.*

*If it wasn't for Sameer, we wouldn't have found the right care and the right medication for you to be in the condition to function. You were non-functional, you couldn't do anything. And because of Sameer and him intervening in your treatment and getting you into the right place, you could function. And it was amazing.*

*The other person I'm grateful for is Mum. Because Mum's always been there to phone the doctor, to phone the pharmacy, to check that you have the medication, to send me to Brighton to make sure you had medication there. Remember that happened as well. We have to thank Mum for always making sure you had the right treatment at the right time. Without Sameer and without Mum, you wouldn't be where you are today.*

*Saying that though. It was all your work. No one got you to this position except yourself. And to think how you did it. Nick mentioned that you didn't attend any of your classes. Now that's one thing. But you did a full-time job at the same time? Talk about insane, which we know you are. But you managed it. And not only that when you managed those things, you were still consistently on a first-class grade, every single term. It was incredible. Plus, you went through a trauma last year. The end of your engagement and a difficult time for us all at the same time. You kept it all together. We are all immensely proud of you.*

*So, the way forward. Because your motivation is brilliant. It isn't money, it's not ego, it's to help your people. Those with mental health problems. And you actually do it. We're immensely proud of you, we look forward to what you're going to do in the future."*

Now, I want to say something. Thank you to all the loved ones out there who support those with bipolar and thank you to all the mental health professionals who try their best to make sure all of us get the right treatment. All of you who are supporting us are beautiful. I realise it must not be easy for you, but I view you all as true heroes. You are the support team and intel for the many with bipolar who are still fighting wars inside their head and in their life right now. Without people like you, I doubt I would be alive today. I hope you can all learn something from this book and that it may help you understand your loved ones or clients a bit better. I hope it will also make you feel appreciated and make you feel that your work is worth it. It truly is.

I count myself as incredibly lucky. It's been a difficult road, but one that has taught me a lot. I've greatly enjoyed writing this book. It's been an amazing journey. Hopefully, my story can help others.

# *References*

Akdede, B. B. K., Alptekin, K., Kitiş, A., Arkar, H., & Akvardar, Y. (2005). Effects of quetiapine on cognitive functions in schizophrenia. *Progress in Neuropsychopharmacology and Biological Psychiatry, 29*(2), 233-238.

Ashok, A. H., Marques, T. R., Jauhar, S., Nour, M. M., Goodwin, G. M., Young, A. H., & Howes, O. D. (2017). The dopamine hypothesis of bipolar affective disorder: the state of the art and implications for treatment. Molecular psychiatry, 22(5), 666-6

Beehr, T. A., King, L. A., & King, D. W. (1990). Social support and occupational stress: Talking to supervisors. *Journal of Vocational Behavior, 36*(1), 61-81.

Brown, B. (2011, October). Shame Perfectionism and Embracing Wholehearted Living. In *Iris* (No. 61, p. 12). University of Virginia.

Ellicott, A., Hammen, C., Gitlin, M., Brown, G., & Jamison, K. (1990). Life events and the course of bipolar disorder. *The American journal of psychiatry.*

Fillingim, R. B., & Blumenthal, J. A. (1992). Does aerobic exercise reduce stress responses?. In *Individual differences in cardiovascular response to stress* (pp. 203-217). Springer, Boston, MA.

Hankir, A. (2011). bipolar disorder and poetic genius. *Psychiatria Danubina, 23,* S62-8.

Harvey, A. G. (2008). Sleep and circadian rhythms in bipolar disorder: seeking synchrony, harmony, and regulation. *American journal of psychiatry, 165*(7), 820-829.

Hardy, D., & Hardy, D. (2019). *The Compound Effect: Jumpstart Your Income, Your Life, Your Success.* Blackstone Publishing.

Flavell, J. H. (1979). Metacognition and cognitive monitoring: A new area of cognitive-developmental inquiry. *American l psychologist, 34*(10), 906.

Funston, L., & Oehler, C., 20 Stress Relieving Foods to Try if You're Feeling Anxious. Retrieved from https://www.health.com/food/stress-relieving-foods?s

Greenwood, T. A. (2016). Positive traits in the bipolar spectrum: the space between madness and genius. *Molecular neuropsychiatry*, 2(4), 198-212.

Jamison, K. R. (2015). *An unquiet mind: A memoir of moods and madness* (Vol. 4). Pan Macmillan.

Kazantzis, N., Fairburn, C. G., Padesky, C. A., Reinecke, M., & Teesson, M. (2014). Unresolved issues regarding the research and practice of cognitive behavior therapy: The case of guided discovery using Socratic questioning. Behaviour Change, 31(1),

Koenders, M. A., Giltay, E. J., Spijker, A. T., Hoencamp, E., Spinhoven, P., & Elzinga, B. M. (2014). Stressful life events in bipolar I and II disorder: cause or consequence of mood symptoms?. *Journal of Affective Disorders*, *161*, 55- 64.

Kruijshaar, M. E., Barendregt, J., Vos, T., De Graaf, R., Spijker, J., & Andrews, G. (2005). Lifetime prevalence estimates of major depression: an indirect estimation method and a quantification of recall bias. European journal of epidemiology, 20(1)

Kupka, R. W., Altshuler, L. L., Nolen, W. A., Suppes, T., Luckenbaugh, D. A., Leverich, G. S., ... & Post, R. M. (2007). Three times more days depressed than manic or hypomanic in both bipolar I and bipolar II disorder 1. Bipolar disorders, 9(5), 531-

Lambert, N. M., Fincham, F. D., & Stillman, T. F. (2012). Gratitude and depressive symptoms: The role of positive reframing and positive emotion. *Cognition & Emotion, 26*(4), 615-633.

Leach, M. J. (2005). Rapport: A key to treatment success. *Complementary therapies in clinical practice, 11*(4), 262-265.

Lim, D., & DeSteno, D. (2016). Suffering and compassion: The links among adverse life experiences, empathy, compassion, and prosocial behavior. *Emotion, 16*(2), 175.

Mammen, O. K., Pilkonis, P. A., Chengappa, K. N., & Kupfer, D. J. (2004). Anger attacks in bipolar depression: predictors and response to citalopram added to mood stabilizers. *The Journal of clinical psychiatry, 65*(5), 627.

Maslow, A., & Lewis, K. J. (1987). Maslow's hierarchy of needs. *Salenger Incorporated, 14*, 987.

Merikangas, K. R., Akiskal, H. S., Angst, J., Greenberg, P. E., Hirschfeld, R. M., Petukhova, M., & Kessler, R. C. (2007). Lifetime and 12-month prevalence of bipolar spectrum disorder in the National Comorbidity Survey replication. Archives of genera

Nabkasorn, C., Miyai, N., Sootmongkol, A., Junprasert, S., Yamamoto, H., Arita, M., & Miyashita, K. (2006). Effects of physical exercise on depression, neuroendocrine stress hormones and physiological fitness in adolescent females with depressive

Perlis, R. H., Smoller, J. W., Fava, M., Rosenbaum, J. F., Nierenberg, A. A., & Sachs, G. S. (2004). The prevalence and clinical correlates of anger attacks during depressive episodes in bipolar disorder. Journal of affective disorders, 79(1-3), 291-

Purcell, M. (2006). The health benefits of journaling. *Psych Central*.

Rausch, S. M., Gramling, S. E., & Auerbach, S. M. (2006). Effects of a single session of large-group meditation and progressive muscle relaxation training on stress reduction, reactivity, and recovery. International Journal of Stress Management, 13(3

Rees, C. S., McEvoy, P., & Nathan, P. R. (2005). Relationship between homework completion and outcome in cognitive behaviour therapy. *Cognitive Behaviour Therapy, 34*(4), 242- 247.

Sandlund, E. S., & Norlander, T. (2000). The effects of Tai Chi Chuan relaxation and exercise on stress responses and well-being: an overview of research. *International Journal of Stress Management, 7*(2), 139-149.

Thorén, P., Floras, J. S., Hoffmann, P., & Seals, D. R. (1990). Endorphins and exercise: physiological mechanisms and clinical implications. *Medicine & science in sports & exercise.*

# *Author Bio*

Samuel Swidzinski is a mental health advocate, academic and author of the new self-help book, 'winning the war with bipolar'. In 2013, following years of turmoil and grief, Samuel received a diagnosis of bipolar 1. He felt fortunate to meet some inspiring psychiatric researchers from King's College, who helped him to manage his disorder and live a meaningful life.

Samuel has now received funding for a PhD at Kings College. There, he will be studying the impacts of Cognitive Remediation Therapy on bipolar disorder.

Samuel has also worked within the mental health field with clients with a range of mental health disabilities, ranging from autism and schizophrenia to personality disorders. The combined value of Samuel's personal, occupational and academic experience in bipolar has inspired him to write a book about it.